THE PRACTICAL GUIDE TO

DOG
AND
PUPPY CARE

A Norwegian Buhund bitch with puppy

A family group of Dalmatians

THE PRACTICAL GUIDE TO

DOG
AND
PUPPY CARE

A superbly illustrated guide to day-to-day
care and training of your dog or puppy

Andrew Edney — Roger Mugford

Tetra Press

No. 16022

A SALAMANDER BOOK

CREDITS

© 1987 Salamander Books Ltd
Published in the USA by
Tetra Press
3001 Commerce Street
Blacksburg, VA 24060

ISBN 1-56465-164-9

Editor: Anthony Hall
Designer: Bob Mathias
Photographs: Marc Henrie, TEKTOFF
— RM/;CNRI/Science Photo Lib (p.47)
Illustrations: Clive Spong
Color origination: Contemporary
Lithoplates Ltd.
Typesetting: AKM Associates (UK) Ltd.

Printed by Proost International Book
Production, Turnhout, Belgium.

AUTHORS

Andrew Edney
Is a graduate of the Royal Veterinary
College, London and also has an
Honours Arts degree. He is a Past
President of the British Small Animal
Veterinary Association, and acts as
veterinary advisor to Pedigree
Petfoods, UK, Animal Studies Centre.
He is a sometime advisor on
Companion Animal Affairs to the
World Health Organization at Geneva,
and Junior Vice-President of the World
Small Animal Veterinary Association.
He is also Chairman of SCAS, The
Society of Companion Animal Studies.
He has been Editor of Pedigree Digest
since 1984, and has written and
contributed to a wide range of
publications on the subjects of dog and
cat husbandry, zoonoses, euthanasia
and clinical nutrition.

Roger Mugford
Is a comparative psychologist with an
enduring interest in the relationship
between people and pets. After
graduating from the University of Hull
in 1969, he joined the Animal Centre
at Waltham-on-the-Wolds. He left in
1977 to set up a referral practice
specializing in treating behavioural
problems of dogs and cats. Since
beginning his practice he has treated
over 9,000 pets and has become well
known in the veterinary profession and
beyond for his work.

CONTENTS

PHOTOGRAPHER

Marc Henrie
Marc began his career as a Stills Man at the famous Ealing Film Studios in London. He then moved to Hollywood where he worked for MGM, RKO, Paramount and Warner Brothers.

Later, after he had returned to England, Marc specialized in photographing dogs and cats, rapidly establishing an international reputation.

He has won numerous photographic awards, most recently the Kodak Award for the Best Animal Photograph and the Neal Foundation Award for Outstanding Photography of Animal Behaviour.

Marc is married to ex-ballet dancer Fiona Henrie. They live in West London with their daughter Fleur, two Cavalier King Charles Spaniels and a cat called Topaz.

US CONSULTANT

Hal Sundstrom
As president of Halamar Inc. Publishers, of North Virginia. Hal Sundstrom has been editing and publishing magazines on travel and pure-bred dogs since 1972. He is the recipient of six national writing and public excellence awards from the Dog Writer's Association of America, of which he is now president, and he is a past president of the Collie Club of America.

Hal has an extensive background and enormous experience in the dog world as a breeder/handler/exhibitor, match and sweeps judge, officer and director of specialty and all-breed clubs, show and symposium chairman, and officer of the Arizona and Hawaii Councils of Dog Clubs.

INTRODUCTION: YOU AND YOUR DOG

Most people who have kept a dog at some time in their lives know that a family seems incomplete without one. Your dog will give you an enormous amount of companionship, love and affection for many years.

For most of us, we also gain a good measure of protection and much-needed support from our dogs in present-day society.

Most people buy a dog for companionship: it is something which is alive and responds to us in a way which objects, though they may be very attractive in themselves, do not. Beautiful books, paintings or pottery, although desirable as objects, are no different for our being there with them. As they do not react to us, we cannot have a normal, loving relationship with them.

Most dogs give us immediate, unstinting and generous love and affection. They undoubtedly enrich our lives and we would be very poor without them. Whatever other objects we collect around us, dogs hold a very special place.

Assessing the cost

Another consideration is the family budget. As a member of the family, a dog is entitled to a part of the family's financial resources. In short, it is bound to cost something to keep and feed another living being in the household. Just to introduce a dog into the home and expect the costs to be absorbed without any effect on anything else is naive, just as it would be to do the same for a new baby in the family.

The daily costs are not great for most dogs, but they are continuous and will go on for some 10 to 15 years and, with luck, even longer. The actual cost of buying a dog, although an important consideration, is small spread over the average lifetime of most such pet animals.

Once the decision has been made and the time and effort required is set aside for the care

Above: *Dogs can be protectors as well as good companions.*

of a dog, then the rewards are very great indeed. But to get the best out of the partnership, there are many matters which need to be considered.

Assessing the dog

The most obvious point to look at, after it has been decided that the circumstances allow proper attention to adding a dog to the household, is the type of dog best suited to the family's circumstances.

Should it be a purebred or crossbred? What size, what type and which breed should it be? Active or passive, hairy or short-haired, a good guard dog (either as a warning and burglar alarm or a formidable anti-burglar device), male or female? Should you take on a puppy or would an adult be better?

There are points for and against all these options, but to be able to make the best decisions you will need to know the main characteristics of as many types of dog breed as possible. Then you need to assess your own circumstances to see how they fit together.

The human-dog bond

If we look at the relationship between ourselves and our pet

Below: *Training a Gundog needs a good sense of teamwork.*

Above: *Very often, dogs help us to break down social barriers.*

animals dispassionately, or as nearly so as we can, it seems strange that one species, humans, should keep another, dogs, to share its home. Dogs are certainly not humans, but we tend to treat them as such.

We are attracted to their facial appearance, especially when they have eyes which can look at us as directly as those of a child. We get comfort from the touch of their fur. The very act of stroking a dog is known to have a calming effect. This contact with the dog's coat has been shown to reduce raised blood pressure, and recent work has shown that survival after heart conditions is greatly improved by owning a dog.

We give dogs names, and talk to them as if they actually understood our language. There is much to gain from confiding in a canine friend which will never betray us or will never take a disagreeable attitude to what we try to express. Dogs are certainly very quick to understand something of what we mean, but that is usually clear from the way we say the words we use and how we behave in terms of what is known as 'body language'.

We do not have to know any of the Japanese language to understand when a Japanese man or woman is angry and threatening, or happy and pleased to see us. They can make it very clear that what we do is to their liking or not, without the need for us to have any idea of what the words mean.

So it is that our dogs 'read' us very well indeed, and as they are mostly very anxious to please us, they anticipate our actions with great skill. We tend to forget that we are always giving out signals which tell our dogs what is likely to happen. As an example, it is quite clear to a dog when we are making preparations for going out for a walk or getting a meal ready.

Much less obvious actions can

be every bit as clear to a dog, which has the opportunity to watch its owner and the family for many hours each day. The dog usually has no trouble anticipating what we are going to do and when.

Unlike most mammals, which can express a great deal from their body language, dogs also use their very mobile facial expression. This range of movement allows at least six different emotions to be expressed.

A dog in the family

Dogs are very social animals; that is, they thrive in groups. A dog sees its own social group as the pack, in which there is a well-established hierarchy, popularly known as the 'pecking order'. The pack does not have to be all of the same species, and in the human home the whole family is the 'pack' as far as the dog is concerned.

What is crucial to a happy home is that the human owner is the 'pack leader' and does not allow the dog to behave like a spoilt child. Just as a spoilt child is not a happy child, the dog which has its own way all the time can make everyone's life a misery.

This does not mean that an owner has to be so dominant that aggression or even cruelty is needed to maintain dominance. A much gentler and subtle way is all that is required. The chapter 'Feeding and Care' develops this subject in more detail.

In addition to the health benefits to heart patients already mentioned, the dog can help maintain physical health in a more direct way by encouraging an owner to take regular outdoor exercise. Less obvious is the fact that as dogs need attention and food every day, so older owners who might otherwise neglect themselves tend to make special efforts on account of the dog, from which both parties benefit. Left alone, retired people may not get any provisions into the house or even keep it warm and dry, if it were not for the fact that they have another living thing to care for and consider.

Dogs can act as a remedy for loneliness outside the house as well as in private. A friendly and attractive dog acts as an 'icebreaker' in situations where it might be difficult to talk to anyone. Most people find that the

Above: *A guide dog can bring a new feeling of independence.*

Left: *Ever alert, Border Collies are perfect work dogs.*

company of a well-behaved dog allows them to make friends with a variety of passers-by in public places, without any other cause for them to become acquainted.

Dogs are the perfect subjects in conversations with casual acquaintances or total strangers who would not consider striking up a conversation in other circumstances. The dog even allows for conversations to be ended without embarrassment if this is needed. Dogs give an owner more confidence, independence and self-esteem.

This is especially so with guide dog owners. Not only do their dogs help them along the road, but they reduce the need for reliance on the help of others but at the same time the dog helps the blind person to make more friends.

Dogs and child development

There is even a hidden educational role for the dog in the family where there are small children. It is easier to demonstrate biological functions such as growth and development, toilet activities and reproduction when these can all be seen in the dog in the home.

It can be shown to a child that the dog may be reprimanded effectively without violence and that it will still be loved afterwards, even though it may have been naughty. Censure for one matter can be shown not to be universal condemnation and rejection.

There are some benefits from learning about parting and bereavement from a relatively short-lived animal; this can stand a child in good stead later on for coping with the inevitable family deaths.

An only child can gain much benefit from the companionship of a playmate dog which is always around to join in the everyday adventures of the child's world. It has been shown recently that a child with a pet animal is held in greater esteem by schoolfriends, and that a child will confide in its dog more than any other individual.

A healthy respect and love for dogs and other pet animals can certainly improve pet ownership later in life, as the early experiences are freely drawn upon. A child who has owned a dog is almost certainly going to be a dog owner as an adult.

CHOOSING AND BUYING

Having decided that the circumstances are suitable for having a dog in the home, a whole series of questions then arise on how this can be done. The most important are: how to select a breed best suited to the new owner, and then how to find an individual dog which is the best possible example for the home where it will live.

The environment

A good home environment is vitally important for a contented dog. The type of house and area where it is located are relevant. Flats or apartments tend to have the least space, and detached houses the most. Terraced and semi-detached houses come in between. Similarly, a country house is more likely to be able to accommodate a dog than one in a town centre. Other urban and suburban houses come in between.

There will, of course, be plenty of notable exceptions to this rule. Some city centre apartments may be very spacious and a few rural, detached houses may be cramped and not very suitable for dogs. These are merely points to review as they will influence the decisions made. So also is the amount of garden or open space available for exercise.

A very small garden may not be a handicap if there are plenty of open spaces within easy walking distance. Nearby public open spaces will be no use, however, unless the new owner provides regular walks to take full advantage of them. The large garden, meanwhile, retains its advantages only as long as the owner is not a meticulous gardener who cannot tolerate anything likely to damage revered plants.

Even if the local park or open space is not all that near, an owner who is willing to take some time and trouble, and make good use of what there is, can still

Above: *A small garden can be used effectively for exercise.*

enjoy the company of an active dog. All this is provided the local authority allows access for dogs.

Having considered the geography of the house and its surroundings, a few points about the people in the house need to be looked at. The age group of the new owner and his or her degree of everyday activity are obvious points. It is also important to take into account the presence of aged or infirm members of the family.

No-one would want to endanger members of the family who are not capable of protecting themselves from a boisterous dog. Equally, some dogs are not best suited to a home where there are small children, although much will depend on how the children behave and on how the dogs have been brought up. Dogs that have always known the ways of tiny infants or exuberant teenagers are better suited to coping than those that have not, whatever the breed of dog.

What sort of dog?

Once the environment and the people in it have been looked at, the next points to examine relate to the dog itself. What is the preferred size range: is the potential owner thinking of a toy (2-5 kg/4-11 lb) dog, or a large breed (50-100 kg/110-220 lb) or something in between, such as a small (10-20 kg/22-44 lb) or a medium (20-50kg/44-110 lb) breed?

The same applies to the level of activity in the dog. Is a gentle, somewhat lethargic breed favoured or a very energetic and boisterous little dynamo? There are many reasonably quiet and plenty of fairly lively breeds in between.

The type of coat is a most important consideration. Very hairy dogs such as Old English Sheepdogs or Afghan Hounds may look attractive when beautifully turned out at a show but unless an owner is prepared to put in a good deal of effort in every day of the dog's life, the animal will not only look untidy, but will probably be unhappy as well. Its matted fur will feel uncomfortable, and the dog's life

Left: *The sheer variety of dog breeds can complicate choice.*

15

will be the worse for all the torment of unsuccessful attempts at grooming.

Whether the coat is short, medium or long, wiry or soft, it will make a good deal of difference to what turns out to be suitable or unsuitable for the household.

Whether the puppy is a male or female is a matter of choice. The advantages of bitches are that you can breed from them (if this is what you wish) and that they tend to be more home-loving and less likely to wander off. In general, bitches are a little less boisterous. Male dogs tend to be a little more outward-going as companions.

Bitches come into season about twice a year and measures need to be taken to control the upheaval this can cause either by careful confinement, chemical suppression or surgical neutering.

Many owners need a dog that will help protect them, so for them the dog's ability to be a guard matters a great deal. Some owners may want a dog that merely acts as a 'burglar alarm',

and many breeds are very effective as just that. Others with more pressing needs may want a formidable guard dog.

Cost considerations
Lastly (though it might be as appropriate to make finance the first point to take into account) the amount of the family's resources which the new dog owner is prepared to set aside is of crucial importance. Anyone who is not prepared to commit some monies to the maintenance, health and welfare of a dog should consider something else as a pastime.

The cost of actually buying a good specimen is the first, but by no means the only consideration. A dog will need vaccinating and possibly neutering. Vaccinations must be boosted annually. Proper health and veterinary care is essential, and this is best covered by pet insurance. This should also include third party liability as we are all responsible for our dogs.

Table 1 shows the main cost considerations of owning a dog.

Above: *Crossbred puppies may not be predictable as adults.*

Left: *Rottweilers have great reputations as guard dogs.*

Neglecting third party liability can result in some fairly hefty fees or legal penalties, in certain circumstances, although some household policies do cover this type of risk as well.

Purebred or crossbred?
Not everyone wants a purebred dog and in some ways crossbred individuals can be very appealing. However, it is impossible to predict how a crossbred puppy will develop if its ancestry is unknown. Even when the dog is of one known breed crossed with another, it can be something of a gamble how it will turn out.

Even purebred dogs are not totally predictable in this way, but the breed characteristics and the nature of the mother and father give a very strong indication of the potential there is for developing into the sort of dog the new owner wants.

Adult or puppy?
It may be possible to obtain an adult dog rather than a puppy. There are some obvious advantages, as the puppy stages have passed and the adult nature of the dog is evident. But it is vital

---

TABLE 1: THE MAIN COSTS OF KEEPING DOGS

Original purchase price
Vaccination and annual boosters
Anti-worm treatment
Insurance against accident and illness
All veterinary fees not covered by insurance
Cost of a neutering operation or:
    boarding of bitches during oestrus or:
    chemical prevention of oestrus
Food every day of the dog's life
Accessories such as collars, leads and bedding
Shampoos and external anti-parasite preparations
Boarding charges during holidays and emergencies

to consider why the dog has become available; when discovered, the reason may turn out to be a powerful argument against taking the dog on.

Sources

The usual and the most reliable source of healthy dogs is the dog breeder. These are people who devote a good deal of their lives to breeding from their own stock and rearing puppies for sale. Breeders therefore offer the best chance of fulfilling the needs of potential dog owners who are seeking a new pet.

Many dog breeders are active in the world of showing, which has as its main purpose the exhibition of individual dogs which are nearest to what is judged to be a standard of perfection for each breed of dog. The conscientious and caring breeder is therefore deeply concerned with producing and maintaining sound stock.

Equally, breeders who have the welfare of the breed and their own dogs as a matter of concern, will be anxious to make sure the dogs bred from their kennels always go to homes where they will be well cared for.

It is up to the new owner to take the greatest care in selecting a breeder of healthy, happy dogs. In the same way the new owner must expect to be asked a few pertinent questions to reassure the breeder that each puppy will be properly looked after.

The final decision on the actual breed of dog may take a long time to complete. It helps a lot to visit a large dog show where all the popular breeds of dog can be seen together in one place, usually in quite large numbers. It is then possible to make an assessment of how a particular breed will fit into the household for which it is intended.

This is much better than picking a dog just because it looks 'cute' without another thought on how it will adapt to a particular home. It is also more effective than

reading accounts of the characteristics of breeds from a book. This is especially so when the descriptions have been written by fanciers who may not recognize any inadequacies in 'their' breed and record only a eulogy for their favourite.

Dog breeders can be contacted at the shows, but normally their attention is taken up with the business of the exhibition. A follow-up telephone call and visit can easily be made afterwards. Alternatively, the weekly and monthly dog magazines are full of information on puppies which are or will be available. The Kennel Club can normally provide the address of the breed club which will have all the information on breeders in any locality.

Any friend who has the breed desired will also usually be happy to provide particulars on the source of their puppy.

Visiting the breeder

The investment in a puppy is a long-term one, that is, the actions

taken will affect the whole family for ten to fifteen years or even more. A lot of care is needed to make sure the right decisions are made. There are certain guidelines which, if followed carefully, are more likely to lead to a happy result than if an owner does not think ahead a little.

The first move is to telephone or write for an appointment to see all the puppies for sale at each kennel. It is best to try to see all possible puppy candidates before making the final decision, rather than just forming an attachment with the first one seen. If, however, a selection is made without seeing all the puppies, the normal rules of courtesy apply and appointments not required must be cancelled.

It is a mistake to take the children along, as it is too easy to spend the time watching the behaviour of your own family when attention needs to be directed towards the puppies and their environment. It is also much more difficult to come away from

a kennel without a puppy which may not be exactly right.

By visiting several breeders it is possible to form an opinion of the general standard of care and hygiene. First impressions are usually very telling. It is a mistake to expect a breeding kennel to look like a surgical ward, but a little experience soon enables anyone to tell the difference between the 'lived in', moderate dishevelment of a busy kennel, and the squalor and neglect of a badly-run establishment.

The same applies to the general behaviour of the dogs and puppies. It is quite reasonable for all the dogs in a kennel to bark a lot when visitors arrive, but it can be very irritating if it persists and prevents any sort of conversation. If most of the dogs look happy and healthy, the signs are encouraging.

A few individuals may look quite old. If this indicates a

Below: *Breeders take care about their puppies' futures.*

potential for longevity, then this is an advantage too. If, on the other hand, there does not seem to be a healthy young dog in the place, then further investigation is indicated, and if necessary, a move on somewhere else.

The age of the puppy should also be discovered, as taking on a puppy before eight weeks can be a real risk. Whether a male or female is preferred should be made clear too. It is important to look very carefully at at least one of the puppy's parents, particularly from the point of view of temperament. A bitch may still look a little run down having reared a litter, but she should show the sort of disposition the new owner is looking for.

Buying the puppy
It is most important to establish exactly what the fee for the puppy includes and what it does not include, and when the new puppy can be taken to its new home.

Most purebred puppies will have a pedigree certificate and possibly a registration transfer form if they are registered with the Kennel Club. A vaccination certificate will also be available if protective injections have been given.

It is absolutely crucial to know exactly what injections have been given and what remain to complete the course of vaccination. If there is any doubt at all, it will have to be assumed that the puppy is not protected by any vaccinations.

It does not take a great deal of skill to notice if a puppy is bursting with health or is looking very sick. It may however, look and act as if it were very uncomfortable if picked up by a stranger. Its mother may react in an anxious way as well. So it is best to examine puppies without their mother there and without too much manipulation.

It is most important to ignore all excuses intended as

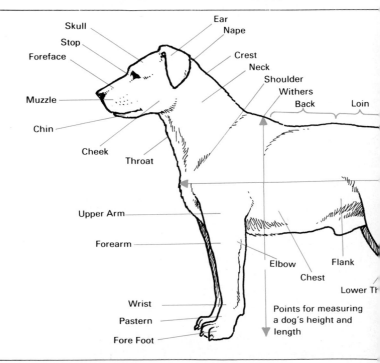

Skull
Ear
Nape
Stop
Foreface
Crest
Neck
Shoulder
Withers
Back
Loin
Muzzle
Chin
Cheek
Throat
Upper Arm
Forearm
Elbow
Flank
Chest
Lower Th
Wrist
Pastern
Fore Foot
Points for measuring a dog's height and length

'explanations' of a puppy's poor appearance. If there is some doubt, a puppy said to be a little 'off colour' can be seen another day. If it is not quite right then, it is best avoided. It is wise for the new owner to give the proposed new addition to the household a thorough check before the purchase is finalized.

It is not always the best strategy to go for the most forward puppy unless that is the type wanted as an adult. Equally it is a mistake to pick out one which cowers in a corner and is not well socialized with its littermates.

Above all, it is very unwise to select a puppy out of pity. Simply feeling sorry for a weakly individual is a recipe for a life of continuous problems for many years.

The last item to check is what the puppy has been fed on since it was weaned. A detailed account of the diet is most useful, even if a quite different regime is planned for the rest of its life. Sudden changes of diet are likely to cause digestive upsets, so any new feeding plan needs to be introduced slowly. It is best to find out about feeding methods from the local veterinary surgeon when other matters such as vaccination, worming and neutering are discussed.

All documentation should be available when the puppy is collected. Beware of paperwork which will be 'sent on'. It is wise to get such promises in writing or at least to leave a stamped, addressed envelope to improve the chances of this happening. Don't risk being fooled.

Other sources

It is possible to obtain a puppy or an adult dog from a variety of other sources and many happy relationships start in this way. However, the chances of success are less, the less is known about the animal being taken into the household. Friends and neighbours often have bitches with litters and provided the same sort of care is taken as with any breeder, then there is a good chance of success. Retired Greyhounds usually make particularly good pets once they become too old to race and their competitive careers are over.

Pet shops, police or animal welfare society pounds are more of an unknown quantity. Clearly it is unlikely that much will be known about the animal's ancestry and it will not be possible to have any idea of what the puppy's parents or litter mates were like.

Many such organizations do, however, take as much care as they possibly can to reduce the chances of a misfit dog being recycled. The more remote the person who actually bred the dog is from the buyer, the more pitfalls there are for the unwary purchaser and the more vital the advice of a veterinarian becomes.

THE POINTS OF THE DOG
These are the names by which areas of the dog are known.

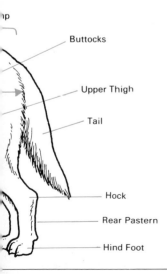

ıp

Buttocks

Upper Thigh

Tail

Hock

Rear Pastern

Hind Foot

YOUR DOG AT HOME

Dogs which share human homes have to have some arrangements made for fitting them into the household environment. An important consideration, too often forgotten, is the need for a refuge from the general hurly-burly of everyday life in the house. Typically, this is where the dog's basket or bed would be situated.

Each dog should have an area set aside as its alone. This is particularly important when there are small children about who need to be told that this is territory for the dog. It becomes even more of a priority if the animal is very young and has just been introduced into the household.

An effective way of introducing a puppy into the household is to set up a small playpen to keep it confined for a few days to get it used to the home scene. This is even more useful if there is an adult cat well established on the strength. It also serves to distance inquisitive infants for a while.

The location of the refuge should be somewhere dry and draught-proof. If, as it often is, it is in the kitchen, it should be well clear of human traffic and away from the hazards of cooking and heating.

Beds and bedding
The size and degree of activity of the dog will dictate the dimensions of the bed. The most important feature should be enough room for the dog to turn itself around in. A metal-framed wooden bed set a few inches off the ground works very well but others may prefer a basket. Anything made out of cane tends to get chewed and is difficult to clean but often serves an older, quieter dog very well. A waterproof lining to go under the blankets is a useful addition.

The blankets themselves do not have to be too luxurious and for the animal's puppyhood, material which can be considered expendable is preferred until the

Above: *Dogs need a refuge of their own where they can feel safe and secure.*

Above: *Beanbags are popular with many dogs, though they must be big enough.*

chewing and wetting stages are passed. Some specially designed blankets are easily washed and are robust enough for almost all dogs. Adult dogs usually take very well to what are known as beanbags. Although they are not always very easy to keep clean they are very relaxing.

It is very necessary to keep all bedding as clean as possible, especially where there are small children about or the dog spends much of its time around the kitchen. A suppy of clean bedding has to be kept available for frequent changing and to allow for the occasional 'accident'.

Collars and leads
Every dog requires a suitable collar and lead. There are many

Above: *Modern accessories make it much easier to control most types of dog.*

Above: *If used, choke chains must be fitted properly to avoid injury to the dog.*

different types of collar available but a simple good-fitting leather one is quite adequate for almost all purposes. Chains and harnesses have their adherents but they do the job no better than an ordinary leather collar, and may be less effective or unsafe if misused.

By the time a puppy has just been weaned, it should already have been introduced to a light collar. This needs to be adjusted very frequently, as puppies are growing at a very fast rate during their first months.

The collar must not be so loose that it could slip over the animal's ears, as puppies nearly always pull back when they first experience a collar. Neither must there be any danger of

strangulation. So the difference between a collar that fits exactly, and one that is either too tight or too loose, is not very great. Because of this, the fit has to be inspected at least every day.

Another reason for frequent collar inspection arises when there are several dogs in the household, as puppies often like to chew the collars of their companions.

Leads can be made of metal or leather, and again the leather variety is quite adequate for most pet owners to use, provided they keep a close eye on any deterioration. A lead that snaps can cause a disaster, so it should be inspected every time the dog goes out for a walk.

Several types of clip attachments are available for the end of the lead. With each of them there is a slight risk of the dog catching the web of its forepaw in the metalwork as it walks or plays. Leads should therefore be kept away from feet. This problem usually arises only when a dog plays with its lead. However engaging it may seem to see a dog frolicking away with a lead in its mouth, it is safer to avoid the slight risk.

A very useful addition to the dog's leatherwear is an extending lead. This allows the dog a great deal of freedom while some degree of remote control is maintained. In the event of any potential hazard coming into sight, the owner retains enough control to take in most of the lead and bring the dog under close attention.

Exercise
There is more to exercise than activity of the muscles. If that was all that was needed, then a running machine would do. Just allowing a dog the run of a garden, however extensive, is still not enough. Dogs need to explore, they need new stimuli to enrich their lives. They need to be taken out. Just letting them out onto the

streets is inviting trouble both for the dog and the owner, not to mention the neighbours.

The commitment to exercise a dog is a very great one. The animal which has no regular new experiences is unlikely to be a happy one and will eventually become a behavioural problem. That is, it can become both a nuisance and a hazard. Exercise should be regular and interesting for dog and owner, rather than an attempt to find the physical limits of either party.

Keeping only to a set walk may improve the chances of the dog getting any exercise at all, but there is a strong chance that the dog will regard all the well-trodden terrain as his own, carefully marking it at frequent intervals and defending it vigorously. Too set a walk can become something of a drudge for the owner as well.

Bad weather will inevitably restrict activities on some days and prevent them altogether from time to time. Some variety in the types of exercise, such as

longer and shorter paths to tread, and the occasional completely new adventure, will be appreciated by most dogs. If you can find an area for the dog to run free, provided it is well enough trained and under reasonable control, then both dog and owner can expect to be happier and healthier as a result.

As most dogs are social animals they are much more active and interactive in small groups. So taking more than one dog out is better for all, provided they are compatible and reasonably controllable. As 'pack leader', an owner must always direct operations, otherwise all outside activity will very quickly get out of hand.

It is often thought that size alone dictates the amount of exercise a dog needs. In fact some very large dogs, such as Saint Bernards, are fairly inert when it comes to energetic movement, and a tiny Jack Russell or Cairn Terrier may not want to go home when all the humans are practically all in.

Above: *Control is needed even when your dog is running free.*

Left: *New experiences help to enrich the lives of our dogs.*

It is very unwise to try to force a dog to be more active than it wants to be. This is rarely a difficulty encountered with young dogs, but as they age, or if they are unwell, they are bound to slow up. A young dog of an active breed which has little interest in exercise is a subject for veterinary attention.

Clearly, working and hunting dogs are more likely to be energetic than more sedate breeds. It is not just a matter of size and bulk.

Cleanliness

All dogs need to relieve themselves, all pass urine and faeces (stools). Although toilet training is covered elsewhere, it cannot be stressed too much that all waste products of dogs, and of other pet animals for that matter, must never be allowed to be a hazard or a nuisance to people or other animals.

It is not difficult to achieve this if a little care and forethought are put in. Getting a dog to relieve itself on command is easy enough, and once this has been achieved you have complete control over where the urine and faeces finish up. It is most inconsiderate and anti-social to use public parks and other open spaces as lavatories.

Getting a dog to relieve itself in the gutter, in a place away from as much human activity as is possible, allows owner and dog to be free in the park afterwards. If the owner uses one of the devices widely available for collecting and disposing of faeces (so-called poop scoops), so much the better.

Alternatively, if the garden is large enough, a dog can be trained to pass urine and faeces before it leaves the owner's premises. A shovel or old newspaper allows the remains to be cleared away.

Most people find all animal waste products aesthetically unpleasant, far beyond the small health hazard they represent. Carelessness in this regard does more to alienate the wider public from pet owners than any other single factor.

Boarding out

There are three basic reasons for boarding a dog out in a kennel. Family holidays are the most obvious and the easiest to plan for. Bitches coming into season (oestrus) are often put into a boarding kennel for security purposes when they are not intended for breeding.

The third possibility is when some emergency arises in the life of the owner, and there is no one to look after the dog, or nowhere else for the dog to go, while the crisis is being resolved.

So the most likely reason for boarding out is the easiest to foresee, and yet often the dog is the last consideration when making holiday plans. The first thing to decide when planning a holiday is not where to go but who in the family is likely to go. The dog is as much part of the family in this respect as any other individual.

Dog owners living in Britain and Ireland must remember that dogs and many other animals must stay behind because of the quarantine laws. Wherever you live, the point to decide is whether to take the dog on holiday or not. If not, then proper arrangements have to be made well in advance.

Leaving a dog in an empty house is definitely inadvisable, even if there might be a neighbour or friend who can help out by feeding and exercising. Anyone so thoughtless as to leave a dog alone in the house like this can expect it to become so bored, frustrated and bewildered that it may leave little of the interior of the house intact on their return. They may well have lost a few friends in the locality, too.

Even getting neighbours to take the dog into their home is asking a lot, as any dog is a considerable commitment and a very good relationship has to exist if this is going to be a success.

There are, however, agencies that offer people who come to live in the house of those who are away on holiday. This is worth further investigation, as it may also provide greater security for the house. Care must be exercised before entering into any such agreements, for very obvious reasons.

Visiting kennels

The golden rules of boarding dogs out are simple. The first is to make firm bookings early. Those who are in the boarding kennel business have to make a living during a few hectic weeks each summer. It is quite unrealistic and selfish to expect the best kennels to be available at a day's notice at the height of the holiday season. The best ones are usually booked solid almost a year in advance.

The second point is to go and have a look at the facilities when making enquiries. It is sheer improvidence to arrive at a kennel for the first time and find that it is quite unsuitable. An inspection does not have to take up a lot of time and need not be too searching. It is usually obvious if the owners are caring, reasonably clean and well organized.

Boarding kennels rarely look like our own homes, nor should they look like hospitals or barrack blocks. They should have a fairly business-like air about them, and the dogs should give the appearance of health and contentment. The best kennels have caring staff and clean, comfortable and secure accommodation for the dogs – so much so that the dogs themselves can enjoy the holiday too.

All bookings must be honoured by both parties: not to show up is about the worst thing an owner can do. Arrangements have to be made for emergencies: where to telephone, and who to call for veterinary help should it be needed, are the most crucial points. Any special feeding or medical requirements have to be made clear. The extent of the kennel's liability should, if

Above: *Good boarding care is always worth paying for.*

Below: *Even half a day is too long to leave a dog on its own.*

possible, be made clear.

Having found a good kennel that takes to a particular dog and *vice versa*, it is best to make the booking here even though this might involve extra time, travel and expense. Paying a reasonable fee is something not to be fudged. A good service merits proper payment. It is silly to come home from your holiday without enough money to pay for the care the dog has had.

Two final points are equally important. All kennels work very hard indeed, especially during the holiday season; it is a demanding way to earn a living. Most of those who are in such a business genuinely care for dogs. They are entitled to some rest after work. It is very unreasonable to expect out of hours service to collect a dog after a late-night return from a holiday trip.

Lastly, any complaints about the service should be made right away on collecting the dog, and preferably to the owner or manager in person – not the kennel maid or other employee. In this way, matters can usually be resolved promptly and without rancour.

27

FEEDING AND CARE

Anything worthwhile is worth looking after. The dogs we have in our homes are quite complicated, much more so than lawn mowers or motor cars. Few of us would expect releatively simple pieces of apparatus just to go on working without some attention now and again. Refuelling, cleaning and servicing, as well as running repairs, are routine requirements with mechanical things. Dogs, being biological organisms of immense complexity, merit at least as much regular attention.

It is very much better to get into a set routine rather than simply reacting (eventually) to matters when they are obviously going wrong. All dogs need to be fed sensibly, that is, 'refuelled'. They must be kept clean by grooming the coat, bathing the dog and attending to the teeth and claws. Regular check-ups, with booster injections to maintain protection against the main killer diseases, are the equivalent of servicing.

Feeding
Of the fundamental requirements of any companion animal, having proper food supplied ranks with equal importance to giving shelter and health care. Owners who are unable or unwilling to give all these to their animals should not even consider taking on such responsibilities.

Having made the commitment to care for a dog, the rewards are great and much pleasure can be derived from the very act of caring. This is especially so when it comes to feeding, as the great majority of dogs look forward to their mealtimes, which provide them with obvious gratification. The supply of food to an animal which is almost entirely dependent upon its owner helps to forge the bond between both.

The other crucial point about feeding is that it has to be done every day of the dog's life. As puppies and in old age, several meals may have to be provided each day.

Types of food
Present-day prepared foods from reputable manufacturers make it a relatively simple matter for owners to meet the nutrient needs of their dogs.

Some dog owners tend to feed a mixture of canned dogfood and a mixer biscuit. Other owners will prefer more of the dry formulations or those with intermediate moisture content.

There are advantages with each format and none is the only 'correct' method of feeding.

Canned foods are mostly very palatable and nutritious, and are preserved by the use of heat sterilization in a closed, very durable container. Dry foods are subjected to heat and kept too dry for micro-organisms to prosper in

Above: *Daily nourishing food is a very important requirement.*

them. They suffer mainly from being less palatable, and will go mouldy if allowed to get wet.

Semi-moist foods come in between and are also heat treated, but preservation is by means of chemicals which prevent the micro-organisms from making use of what moisture there is present.

Dry and semi-moist foods are convenient and can be left down for the dog during the day, whereas canned foods must be eaten within a few minutes or they will dry out.

Left: *Your dog should only be allowed large suitable bones.*

adequate in itself (a complete food) or is meant to be fed with other foods (a complementary food).

How to use prepared foods
There ought to be plenty of information about feeding already printed on the pack of any food from a manufacturer. Most firms also offer background literature for the owner to refer to, and guidance is always available from the local veterinary practice.

Table 2 gives guide to the types of food and the usual amounts to feed puppies during the first months of their development. There is an

Mixer biscuits are very robust and are a cheap source of energy.

All reputable manufacturers give plenty of guidance on how to use the foods they provide. They are required to make it clear on each pack whether the food is

---

TABLE 2: FEEDING PUPPIES

Birth to three weeks: Puppies rely almost entirely on their mother's milk. They feed very frequently and sleep much of the rest of the time.

Three weeks to weaning: Puppies begin to take some solid food, either as canned puppy food designed for the purpose, plus milk or a milk-based weaner food. They should be allowed to eat to appetite in between the periods when their mother allows them to suckle.

Between eight and ten weeks: Puppies are usually weaned from their mother's milk soon after they are two months old. Biscuit softened with milk or water can be introduced and the puppies fed every four hours during a sixteen hour day.
It is at this time that the puppy usually goes to its permanent home and a new routine is introduced.

Weaning to four months: The meal frequency can be gradually reduced from four to three meals per day in the period between three and four months.

Between four and six months: Depending upon the routine which is to be adopted as an adult and on the rate of the dog's development, meals can be reduced to two daily.

After six months: Whatever the adult regime is to be (one or two meals a day), this can gradually be established once the dog is sexually mature. The larger the dog the longer this is likely to take. Very large dogs will be well over a year old before they are fully mature.

enormous amount of variation between the nutrient needs of individual dogs. It is not just that a dog working sheep on a farm will have much greater demands than a fireside dog of the same bodyweight and size. But even dogs which look and behave in a very similar way may vary quite a lot as well.

The right amount

It is up to the owner to make the final judgements on the amounts supplied.. Table 3 gives an approximate guide for adult dogs of different sizes. Fortunately, it is not difficult to judge if a dog is getting too much or not enough food and to make the adjustments in the amounts fed. The difficult matter is actually getting around to doing it.

To continue under- or overfeeding will inevitably lead to problems of either emaciation and scavenging, or obesity. So the dog's health is in the hands of the person who feeds it. If that state of health is prejudiced it will certainly threaten the dog's chances of living a long and happy life.

Different stages of life

Different stages of a dog's life require different feeding strategies.

When a puppy is born it begins to grow very rapidly. If it does not it will not survive. Growth cannot stand still: the puppy will either put on bodyweight or perish. For the first three weeks or so it is entirely dependent upon its mother for nutrients, and it will continue to take milk, and some food that its mother regurgitates for it, until the process of weaning is complete. This may be between the seventh and twelfth weeks of life, or even later in some larger breeds.

Weaning

As the puppies begin to take solid food (see the chapter on birth and growing up, page 56) their needs are at least twice those of a mature dog of the same weight. They have to keep themselves going and grow at the same time. They are bound to need much more per unit bodyweight. They also need to be fed very nourishing, concentrated, easily digestible foods. Even then their stomachs are too small to accommodate enough food for more than a few hours, so they will require meals at very frequent intervals.

Adult dogs vary a great deal also. At one end of the scale a sedentary, fairly lethargic dog does not need very much food just for maintenance, but a bitch rearing a litter is likely to need at

TABLE 3: APPROXIMATE AMOUNTS TO FEED PUPPIES

Size		Small	Medium	Large
Adult Bodyweight:		4.5–9kg (10–20lb)	9–22kg (20–50lb)	22kg (50lb)
Up to 12 weeks:	c/f	½–¾	¾–1	1–1½
	b/m	25–80g (1–3oz)	85–140g (3–5oz)	100–160g (4–6oz)
12–16 weeks:	c/f	½–¾	1–1½	1½–2
	b/m	55–140g (2–4oz)	100–165g (4–6oz)	140–250g (5–9oz)
16 weeks–1 year:	c/f	½–¾	1–1½	1½–2
	b/m	85–140g (3–5oz)	140–225g (5–8oz)	225–335g (8–12oz)

c/f = Canned puppy food   b/m = biscuit/mixer
These amounts are approximate and are meant as a guide. Adjustments can be made on results as there is a great deal of variation between individual dogs.

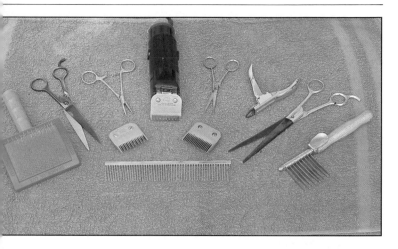

Above: *Regular grooming is easy with the correct equipment.*

Below: *Hound gloves greatly help the grooming routine.*

least three times as much food as this when she is at the peak of lactation (producing milk for puppies).

For dogs doing vigorous exercise such as racing Greyhounds or working farm dogs, at least twice the maintenance level may be needed. The ultimate requirement is for the sledge dog doing very demanding work in very cold conditions.

Older dogs tend to slow down and need less energy from their food, or they may be less efficient at digesting and absorbing food. This often means reverting to the frequent meals of puppyhood, with small amounts of nourishing food provided on a 'little and often' basis. Certainly many of them have a poorer appreciation of food and adjustments will have to be made accordingly (see the chapter on old age).

Grooming

All dogs need grooming, and the sooner the routine is established the easier it is to maintain. Some light brushing should start as soon as a new puppy has had a chance to adjust to its new environment. If this is done for frequent, very short spells, it becomes part of the dog's life and many individuals look forward to the attention they get from their owners.

Grooming must never become a test of the will of dog and owner. A dog that is neglected can become such a trial to de-mat and groom that it may have to be sedated or even fully anaesthetized to complete the task.

A nylon brush, with bristles on one side and metal on the other, is invaluable for regular use. A hound glove, which the owner puts on the hand, is useful for the finishing touches. A metal-toothed comb should deal with most matted areas if there is no

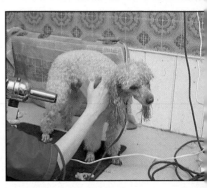

Above: *Most dogs can be washed in a bath or washbasin.*

Above: *A hairdryer can be invaluable after a good bath.*

delay in clearing them as they form.

Each dog should have some old towels which are for canine use exclusively. At least two clean towels should be kept at hand for when the dog comes in on a wet day, or after an encounter with a puddle or two.

Bathing

Just as young dogs have to get accustomed to grooming, bathing has to be introduced in every dog's pattern of life. It is not difficult to bath dogs, no more than it is with small children if the routine is established. Small dogs can usually be bathed in a sink or large washbasin. Larger varieties have to be put into the bath itself or, when the weather is kind, in a tub outside.

Take special care when bathing puppies under six months old, ensuring that they do not take a chill when wet; and in cold weather, dogs of all sizes require this precaution.

Use shampoos that are known to be suitable for dogs. Pet shops and veterinary practices can always provide the right kind. Then it is simply a matter of wetting the coat and applying the shampoo in the same way as any other, taking great care to keep the eyes clear. Rinse out the shampoo, and the dog will be thoroughly washed.

Drying with a hair-drier and a large bath towel is all that is needed to finish off the task. A clean dry towel and a hound glove can be used to finish the job off. A hound glove is a sturdy mitten, made with bristles on the palm side, and is very effective for grooming most dogs.

No dog should be allowed out until completely dry, and everyone should know about the dog's habit of shaking itself dry in a way which makes everyone else around soaking wet.

Any medicated shampoos must be obtained from the veterinary practice and used under guidance to be quite safe. There is no fixed interval for bathtimes, as dogs get dirty at different rates, but it is usually obvious when it needs to be done. Once a month during the summer, plus the occasions when the dog gets in a pickle, is about the par rate; and whenever practicable during colder weather.

Claws

Dogs have a pad and a claw on the four toes of each leg. The main claws are normally just clear of the ground. Many dogs have additional claws on the inside of the leg. These are called 'dew' claws and have very little function as far as most breeds are concerned. They are usually removed (by a vet) very early in the lives of puppies – that is, before the eyes are open, at about ten days.

Some breeds, including the Newfoundland and the Pyrenean Mountain Dog, are allowed to retain them. In these and some other dogs, there are sometimes supernumerary (excess), or double dew claws.

Overgrown claws are usually quite obvious as they will begin to turn over where they touch the ground. The dew claws, if retained, may also overgrow and begin to grow into the pad. This quickly results in a painful wound in the leg which will become infected and needs attention without delay.

One of the main problems with overgrown claws is that, in the hairier breeds at least, it is easy to miss a hidden claw. For this and other reasons of hygiene, it is best to keep the hair short around the feet.

Cutting claws

Many owners shy away from the thought of cutting their dog's claws. If the routine is established from puppyhood, when a small pair of nail scissors is usually enough to take the tips off sharp claws, there should be no difficulty.

The most important factors are that the dog is kept still with the minimum of fuss, and that the

Below: *Care has to be taken when cutting overgrown claws.*

Before

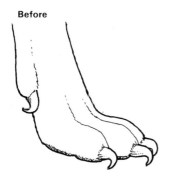

After

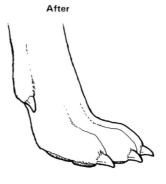

CUTTING CLAWS

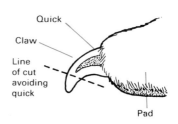

Quick

Claw

Line
of cut
avoiding
quick

Pad

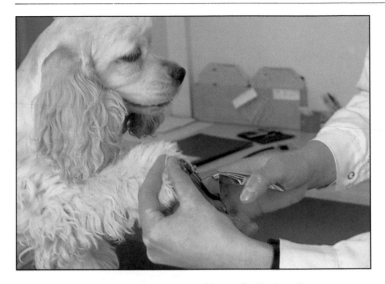

Below: *The ears are just one of the areas for examination.*

Above: *Guillotine clippers are a safer means of cutting claws.*

Below: *It is vital that a puppy has a full series of vaccinations.*

estimate has to be made.

Very long claws are difficult as the quick tends to grow far down the claw. In such cases, clipping is best left to a vet. Otherwise the rule is to keep on the safe side and take off too little rather than too much.

The guillotine type of clippers, used by vets and breeders, is perfectly easy to use, but a substantial pair of ordinary household clippers will suffice for most dogs. The aim is always to restore the claw to the normal position, just clear of the ground.

Check-ups

As vaccination needs to be boosted every year (see page 44) and possibly more frequently in situations where there are increased risks, this provides the basis for a system of regular, routine check-ups. In fact, no vaccine should ever be given to a dog without an examination by a vet, so vaccination boosters automatically entail regular surveillance of the dog's health, without the need for any additional visits to the surgery.

Regular items for the vet's

sensitive 'quick' is avoided, so there is no pain or bleeding. With claws that lack pigment, it is easy to see where the quick is and avoid it, but in many dogs the claw is heavily pigmented and an

AREAS OF EXAMINATION

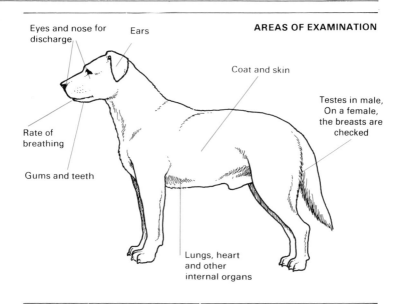

Eyes and nose for discharge

Ears

Coat and skin

Testes in male, On a female, the breasts are checked

Rate of breathing

Gums and teeth

Lungs, heart and other internal organs

annual inspection include the dog's eyes, ears, gums, teeth, skin, body temperature and weight, as well as the functioning of the heart, liver and kidneys. Beyond this, there may be other things that the vet might consider important to monitor in particular cases. The vet should keep careful records, enabling him to compare the findings of each examination with earlier data.

Seeing and checking fit dogs helps the veterinarian, for this means that he does not always see only sick animals. The degree of abnormality of any individual is always easier to judge against what the animal was like when it was well, rather than trying to assess health without any criterion for that individual.

None of this advice means that the owner should not seek professional advice when an emergency arises. Boosters and regular check-ups are quite separate from unforeseen requirements.

Insurance
Keeping animals costs money – not a great deal compared with

Above: *A general examination of a dog covers a number of areas.*

what owners get in return, but the everyday costs of simply maintaining a dog must not be disregarded. You can make an estimate of the day-to-day costs, but this will not cover the bills which inevitably follow accidents or sudden serious illness.

Insurance cover for such events is now widely available. It is sound, household economic sense to protect against the worst, in the same way that it is foolhardy to leave a dog unprotected by vaccination.

Insuring a dog does not cover for vaccinations, boosters or neutering operations, but it will help avoid the shock of a large bill to cope with when there is already the distress of having a sick animal in the household. At the same time you can insure yourself against the costs of any damage your dog may cause to other people or their animals or property. It is always worth checking carefully to make sure that insurance cover is actually sufficient for all these risks.

TRAINING: THE FIRST STEPS

In order to fit into the human household, dogs have to conform to the basic ground rules of the society in which they live. This means that they have to be trained. The dog has to join the group as a member, a very important member but not the dominant one of the household. That is, as far as the dog is concerned, the household is the pack and the owner is its leader.

Dogs live happily in these situations but if any of the humans become subordinate to their dogs, the result is misery for everyone, including even the dogs themselves.

There is more to training than just responding to commands. Dogs which know where they fit into the order of things are able to contribute to the pleasurable, smooth running of life. This certainly does not mean that a dog has to be harshly treated to get it to conform. The great majority of dogs are only too pleased to meet their master's every wish and welcome all opportunities to do so.

Displays of gratification on the owner's part go a very long way to reinforcing the dog's proper position in the hierarchy. The simple withholding of praise has

Below: *Without proper training, dogs can become a nuisance.*

a sufficiently telling effect on a dog to get it to modify its behaviour to try to do better next time around.

Punishment, or any other form of cruelty, is at best useless and inhumane, and at worst very damaging to the relationship between the dog and everyone else in the household.

The basics
There are three main apsects of training dogs to belong in a household. The process begins before a puppy is even weaned, and continues to some degree throughout life.

The first stages of training a dog relate to socialization. This subject is covered in more depth in the chapter on growing up. Basically, the dog has to learn from its relationships with other dogs that it is a dog. Other dogs must be respected as other members of the same species. Any puppy which has no contact at all with others of its kind, and some may never even see their parents, will not know what another dog is if reared in complete isolation.

Equally important to a young dog is the need to learn about the other species with which it is going to come in contact. This is particularly important with the humans in the family. A dog must

Above: *Every dog must learn to fit in with the family 'pack'.*

know that other people in its home command respect. Later on it can be trained to guard against intruders. This respect has to be returned by the family if a proper working relationship is to be developed.

Other pet animals, such as cats or pet rabbits, have to be introduced as friendly, and are not there to be assaulted.

The next stage is toilet or house training, which allows an animal which must, like all others, relieve itself of urine and faeces, to share a home with other species. This must be done in a way which does not present any aesthetic offence or health hazard. In addition, the dog must be trained to avoid risks or nuisance to anyone in the neighbourhood at large, outside its own home.

The obedience part of training does not mean much more than the very basics of getting a dog to walk to heel, 'sit' and 'stay' and to come when called. The advanced standard of training necessary to win prizes in obedience competitions is not essential for owners. Progression to a higher level is best achieved through a dog training club.

Toilet training

All puppies rest and sleep a great deal. They almost always want to relieve themselves as soon as they wake up, so this is the time to begin toilet training. A puppy on arrival in a new home will spend a little time exploring its new surroundings, and then will either go to sleep or look for an opportunity to pass urine or faeces.

It is important not to fuss a new puppy too much on arrival at its new quarters, as there will be an enormous number of new stimuli for it to cope with. It is best to allow it to rest undisturbed to start with. Children, small or

Above: *Toilet training can begin almost immediately.*

large, must be restrained from too much attention or handling to begin with.

An exercise pen fenced off in a part of a reasonably quiet room is useful to begin toilet training. As soon as a puppy wakes up it will normally make it clear that it is about to pass urine or faeces. At this point it will be necessary to pick the puppy up and place it where it is to relieve itself. This may be out in the garden, if there is one, and if the weather is favourable.

Alternatively, it may be more practical to get the puppy to use newspaper until it can be taken out. Owners have to be quite quick to make sure the number of 'accidents' is minimal. The time between indicating and urinating is fairly short but most owners soon learn what the signs are.

The owners have two other duties. The first is to give a very brief command with a one or two word signal. Something like 'go on' or 'be clean' will do. In fact it does not really matter what the words are, as long as they are the same each time. This way any dog can be taught to relieve itself on a single command. This is something which will come in very useful later on.

The other duty is to stay with the puppy until it has finished. After everything has gone as it should, it is necessary for the owner to give the puppy enough praise for it to understand that it has done the right thing. This does not have to be too fulsome, as dogs very quickly learn that what they do is approved or not by their owners. But it should not be mean either. A little expression of satisfaction costs nothing but a little time.

Toilet training is not something which can be put off. The routine is established very early, and if neglected the dog may be impossible, or at least very difficult, to train. Almost as bad perhaps is that it will not be possible to rely on the dog to be clean in the house or to be sure where it will deposit unpleasant material.

The secret with toilet training is to begin early and persevere day in day out, regardless of any 'failures'. After the routine has become established, the failures are usually due to owners' mistakes rather than the dog's.

Collar and lead
Once the dog has its full measure of protection by vaccination (see page 44) then the time has arrived for venturing out. By this time the dog must have been trained to wear a lead. This can begin soon after weaning by fitting a light collar on first, which is kept on for only a few minutes to begin with.

If this is done at a time when the puppy's attention is easily diverted, then it will be tolerated very much better than if the puppy is allowed to protest and struggle to get it off.

Just before meal times is an obvious choice of time to apply the initial lead training. A light-weight lead can be attached for the first few attempts at controlled walking, but the lessons need to be very short to

Above: *A puppy must first get used to the collar and lead.*

begin with. Each lesson should be fun for dog and owner, but not too boisterous, and always with a purpose. Rewarding the dog reinforces the lesson, and withholding praise is all that is usually necessary to make the point with the dog.

Very short walks can be attempted as soon as the dog has come to accept the collar and lead as routine. These *must* be restricted to the garden until the vet gives the all clear to take the dog out: that is, when the course of vaccination is complete.

Obedience training
Teaching the four basic commands can be started before the first excursion outside the home boundaries. As it may be up to 16 weeks or even longer before some dogs are fully protected, it is crucial to start on mastering 'heel', 'sit', 'stay' and 'come' as soon as the puppy has got reasonably used to the collar and lead.

Practice should not interfere with the procedure of toilet training already described. The two activities should be separate lessons in the timetable, at least to begin with.

It is vital that lessons should be short at the outset, as dogs, like small children, are not able to concentrate for very long without getting bored. Later, more prolonged training is required. The work should be fun and not a drudge for either the dog or the owner. It must always have a purpose and an end-point, after which there can be a period of free play to look forward to.

The dog must not be allowed to become exhausted, or the effect may be the opposite to what is wanted. On the other hand, the owner must always be in control and not let the dog dictate when the work starts and finishes.

In quite a short time the dog and the owner should have developed a good working relationship and each will be able to 'read' the other's behaviour with great skill. This interaction is something which improves all the time dog and owner share their lives.

Walking to heel
The discipline of walking to heel starts as soon as the puppy begins to walk on the lead. Puppies usually follow their owners when walking together. In

Above: *'Sit' on command is the next important training step.*

Above: *Walking to heel is best mastered early in a dog's life.*

Above: *Learning to both 'sit' and 'stay' can later save a dog's life in an emergency.*

fact they very soon anticipate the movement and start to pull forward. This has to be curbed straight away, or walks will always be towing operations.

The lead has to be firmly but gently jerked, and the word 'heel' given as the command, so that the puppy has to realize it can be comfortable only when walking at a particular spot at its owner's heel. It should neither drag nor pull. Praise is given when the puppy is in the right place and withheld when it is not. No more than moderate voice indications need be given to make it clear that the puppy is in the wrong place.

Although puppies are usually very quick to catch on, it is important to remember that some individuals are faster on the uptake than others. Too much cannot be expected too soon, and again the lessons should be short and fun. A short free play time, with the collar on but the lead off, can follow each episode of training.

All this training can take place in the garden, if space and weather allow. Alternatively, much can be achieved indoors.

Once walking out is allowed, a quiet spot away from traffic noises and the distraction of other people and dogs should be found, to allow a short period to concentrate on getting some training time in.

As progress is made, then training can become a little more adventurous, but puppies have to get used to traffic and people, so it is most important that the next steps – Sit and stay – are mastered before attempting more advanced training. To neglect this is to expose your puppy to extreme dangers such as traffic or hostile people or animals.

Sit and stay
When not actually moving, a dog should be in a relaxed but alert sitting position when on the lead. Being on the lead will come to be interpreted by the dog as a sign that this is a time to be taken seriously. This does not mean that life cannot be fun. It has to be fun under control.

The 'sit' command is a natural progression from walking to heel. When dog and owner come to a stop, the dog is encouraged to sit by a firm but kindly hand pressing down on the dog's hindquarters. The hand is run down the dog's back so the dog feels a comforting stroking. The pressure is

increased slightly to a maximum across the hips. There is no need at all to create enough pressure to cause pain. Doing so will only alienate the dog and spoil the partnership.

The word 'sit' is said every time the hand is stroked along the dog's back to induce the sitting position. All the words used in training need to be said clearly and must sound as if they are really meant. The same tone should be maintained all the time. There is no need to bark orders, for dogs have very acute hearing. Anything bellowed into their ears is likely to upset them and set the training programme back unnecessarily.

Success is not likely immediately. Even those quickest on the uptake will need a little time to realize that stopping combined with the stroking pressure and the word 'sit' mean just that. Most dogs soon get the idea and as soon as success is achieved, plenty of praise is what is needed. It is not necessary to do any more than make pleasing noises and some gentle stroking.

Small titbits are sometimes given but this may mean that when they are not, the dog may think it has done something wrong. In other words once titbits are started, they will have to be

Above: *Every time at the roadside it is advisable to reinforce the 'sit' command.*

maintained for quite a long time.

Corrections are made by short jerks on the lead. There is no need for violence. Very sharp jerking of the lead may result in damage to the neck, so all training has to be done with kindness and persuasion. However, the owner must remain dominant. When a dog is really truculent and wants to establish dominance over the owner, then it may have to be lifted by the scruff and shaken, to make the point.

Such a move will be seen as something serious by the dog and has to be used very sparingly. Withholding praise is usually enough to get the right result.

Once the sit manoeuvre has been mastered, the dog will have to be taught to stay where it is, wherever the owner goes or whatever he does outside the basic commands. It is not difficult to make progress with this command. The lead can be lifted up as the owner walks around the dog repeating the word 'stay' in a firm but encouraging voice. Every time the dog gets up to see what is going on, the 'sit' position is reapplied.

Above: *An extending lead gives a dog a sense of freedom but also keeps it under control.*

An extension lead makes teaching this part of the programme very much easier. The actual distance away can then be gradually increased until the owner can be quite a long way away and still maintain control over the dog. Every time the dog moves, the word 'stay' is repeated.

When necessary, the owner will have to return to re-establish the sit position. Eventually the dog will come to realize what 'stay' means. It means do not move at all.

Throughout all these operations the only other word which needs to be used is the dog's name. It is added on to each command as a routine.

Come when called

The last of the basic commands which must be learned is 'come'. It allows the owner to keep control over the dog when running free. Again the extending lead is invaluable for increasing the distance the dog is allowed to roam from its owner while still under lead control.

With the dog in the sit and stay position, the dog's name is called

and the lead pulled gently but firmly. A few obvious beckoning movements will help the more reluctant ones, but all that is usually necessary is for the owner to give some praise when the dog comes to command. If the first attempts are unsuccessful, use a shorter lead. Then the lead can be gradually lengthened as progress is maintained.

It is best to make the dog sit as soon as it comes to the owner, as the temptation to jump up and spread muddy paws over the owner is strong in dogs. If the command 'sit' is given as soon as the dog is where it should be, it can be prevented from jumping up before it has a chance to do so.

All training has to be done in short bursts, as a young dog will tire easily and, just as bad, get bored with the whole thing. It is important to realize that it all takes time. It is silly to try to train a dog in a day. Attempts to do so may cause irreparable harm. Patience, perseverance and kindness will achieve it all in the great majority of dogs. Above all, the working together of dog and owner reinforces the bond of love and friendship which will last the rest of the dog's life.

Right: *The command 'come' is always rewarded with praise.*

Above: *Once 'sit' and 'stay' have been mastered it is possible to move on.*

Below: *The 'stay' command is reinforced, before the last command to the dog to 'come'.*

VACCINATION AND NEUTERING

Every right-thinking owner wants to do the very best for their dog. This means protecting it against all the diseases where vaccination is available. In addition to taking the precaution of giving the dog immunity against infectious disease, measures can be taken to prevent unwanted breeding. It is best that all dogs not required for breeding are neutered, in other words have their organs of regeneration removed.

These two topics, vaccination and neutering, are the top priorities for discussion and action at the first visit to the local vet. There is no reason why the subject should not be aired even before taking a dog into the home.

The staff of veterinary practices are used to giving advice on the preferred time for the vaccination programme to begin, the likely cost of the course of injections and the period which will have to be strictly observed before the dog can be taken out.

At the same time, the exact

timing of neutering operations can be explained, and the probable cost of the surgery involved made clear. The new owner can then see what effect these measures will have on the family budget. They are not items to put off until some spare money is available – they are essential considerations.

Vaccination

It has been known for a long time that certain diseases due to micro-organisms cause a reaction in the individual which helps to protect it against further attacks from that particular infectious agent. The technique of vaccination was developed to provoke this response without the disease.

Vaccines do not give the animal the disease, they do not even give the protection directly. What they do is to allow the animal to generate its own protection, that is, to produce an immunity. To do this, the puppy must already be sufficiently healthy and mature in the first place.

This is one reason why the task of vaccination has to be entrusted

Below: *Before each vaccination a health check is given.*

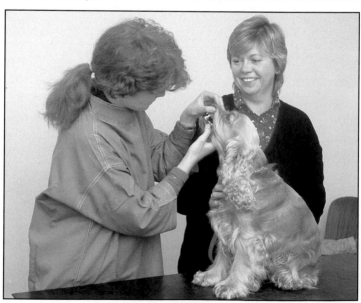

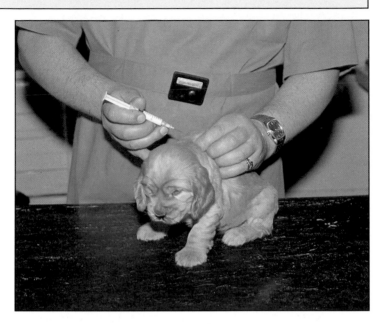

Above: *Protection by early vaccination is vital.*

to a vet, who is qualified to judge the condition of each individual animal before going ahead with the treatment.

Another important reason why the puppy has to be beyond a certain age is that it is normally born with a certain degree of immunity, inherited from its mother. This is known as maternal immunity and during the early weeks it can interfere with the development of a lasting response to vaccination. Maternal immunity is only temporary, and declines rapidly at about the time of weaning.

An extra complication is that for a certain range of diseases, including canine parvovirus disease, the effectiveness of maternal immunity can vary enormously between individual dogs. It may also vary between breeds of dog. The Rottweiler is said to be especially prone to interference in vaccination programmes, caused by immunity inherited from the puppy's mother.

Organizing the programme
The actual timing of the vaccination programme for any puppy will depend on the disease pattern in the neighbourhood. The only person in a position to judge this is the local vet, so it is particularly important for a new owner to make contact with the local practice to see what the situation is. In any case it is crucial that a new puppy does not go out of the confines of the house and garden until clearance is given by the vet attending it.

Most owners take possession of a new puppy when it is between eight and ten weeks old. It may be as young as six weeks but this can cause problems in later life. Waiting until 12 weeks is very much better, but this obviously imposes a strain and extra costs on the breeder, as the puppies grow rapidly, become boisterous and eat a lot.

Whatever the age on acquisition, all new owners must discover what each puppy has had by way of vaccination and, even more important, what is still needed to complete the protection required.

If the vaccination has been completed, there will be a certificate signed by a veterinary surgeon. If this is not available, it will have to be assumed that there is no protection at all and a course of injections will need to be started from the beginning.

Some vets maintain separate vaccination clinics, isolated from the rest of their premises, to make sure the unprotected puppies and kittens are kept away from infection as much as possible. A telephone call or a visit to the practice, without the puppy, will enable you to establish the details of what to do and when.

On no account must an unprotected puppy be allowed to mix with other dogs until the course of treatment has been completed.

Rabies

The rabies disease is the worst fear of dog owners in many countries and can kill dogs, with extremely unpleasant symptoms, while presenting a fearful hazard to public health.

In Britain and other rabies-free countries, it is usually not permissible to use rabies vaccines except in quarantine kennels. However, many countries have to live with rabies and so the vaccine is more readily available in these places. In many countries that are not free from the disease, protection against rabies is compulsory.

Vaccination Programme

No vaccine is 100 percent sure of protecting all dogs in all cases, but thankfully failures are rare, and at least no dog suffers ill effects from the vaccine itself. The possible exception to this is the very occasional individual which is actually allergic to a component of the vaccine. Even this is now rare, since modern vaccines are produced to extremely high standards of purity.

Fear of an allergic reaction should never prevent an owner from protecting his puppy or dog.

Table 4 shows a generalised vaccination programme. This can, however, vary from area to area.

Other main diseases

Canine distemper and hepatitis are both virus diseases caused by micro-organisms too small to be seen with a light microscope. Both are highly infectious and cause a wide range of severe clinical signs.

Treatment is often unrewarding and usually lengthy. It is very frustrating as well, as the dog may appear to get better, only to relapse just as hopes were rising.

Two forms of leptospirosis commonly afflict dogs of all ages. These are caused by bacteria which may also affect humans. In man, the diseases are usually a result of rat contamination and not of contact with dogs.

What is known as kennel cough is a complex of diseases, one of which is related to infection with a species of bacteria known as *Bordetella*. It is possible to give some protection against this illness by vaccination, and any dog likely to be kennelled is best given a course of vaccination for this disease.

While it is perfectly true that other organisms are also connected with kennel cough, this should not be taken as a reason to neglect vaccination against *Bordetella*.

Booster injections

As dogs, like all other animals, are biological systems and not pieces of machinery, they do not all react or behave in the same way. Cases do occur (though extremely rarely) when a dog is completely unable to develop an immunity; on the other hand, there are many dogs that respond to vaccination by setting up an immunity that lasts for several years.

It can be a very devastating

Right: *The deadly Rabies virus shown × 19,000 its actual size.*

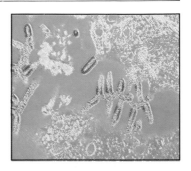

experience for a family to find that the dog's immunity has waned to the point that the dog develops one of the diseases against which it was previously protected.

It is quite wrong to assume that older dogs do not get the killer diseases like canine distemper. This belief arose in the days before widespread vaccination: dogs that were at all susceptible to distemper would normally catch it while still young, as they would inevitably become exposed to the disease early in life.

The belief that immunity is permanent is equally wrong. The actual rate of decline of the immunity is impossible to determine without a blood test.

There is not much point in going to the trouble of bloodtesting a dog if immunity can be easily boosted by a simple injection every year. So single booster injections are given as a matter of routine, to ensure that the degree of protection does not fall dangerously low.

Again, the local vet is the person to advise on the timing for

TABLE 4: USUAL VACCINATION TIMETABLE

Age of puppy	Protection against disease
6–9 weeks	First Canine Distemper combined with first Canine Hepatitis and first Canine Parvovirus Disease injection. First combined Leptospirosis injection
Around 12 weeks	Second Canine Distemper combined with second Canine Hepatitis and second Canine Parvovirus Disease injection. Second combined Leptospirosis injection
	First Rabies vaccine given in countries where the disease is established
14–16 weeks	Second Rabies injection given in countries where the disease is established
16–20 weeks	Third Canine Parvovirus Disease injection where indicated
Annually	Single booster injection of Canine Distemper/Canine Hepatitis/Parvovirus and Leptospirosis required every year to maintain protection

The ages of puppies given are approximate and it must be left to the veterinarian to judge the exact timing of all protective vaccinations.

boosters. Most practices send out reminders when the injections are due. This is also a convenient way to give each dog an annual check-up so that its complete health can be carefully monitored regularly.

Almost all boarding kennels insist on seeing an up-to-date vaccination certificate for their guests, so it is necessary to make sure that the dog's documents are always taken to the surgery and updated at the time of the annual

Below: *The reproductive systems of the male and female dog.*

appointment for a booster and check-up.

Neutering
Dogs are quite a prolific species but the continual production of puppies at every opportunity would not be good for the bitch, for dogs in general or for those of us who have to live in the same environment. It is quite wrong to believe that having a litter is of some benefit, in itself, to the bitch. Any thought of breeding simply because it is 'good for' a bitch should be extinguished from the minds of all dog owners.

MALE REPRODUCTIVE SYSTEM

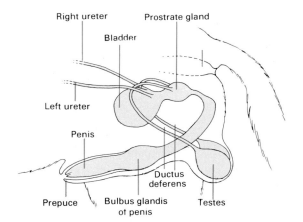

FEMALE REPRODUCTIVE SYSTEM

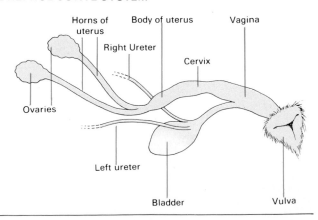

Those dogs required for breeding are a different matter entirely and are dealt with in the next chapter. Here the advice is to neuter all those dogs that are not intended as breeding stock, and at the very least the bitches. The operation of neutering a bitch is called spaying and consists of removing the uterus or womb, and the ovaries.

The result is that the bitch is no longer fertile, cannot produce eggs and is thus unable to conceive and have any puppies afterwards. In addition, as the ovaries are taken out the means of bringing the bitch into season or oestrus is also removed.

The owner has a multiple benefit, as the bitch no longer attracts all the males in the locality, nor runs off to find a mate; neither will she make messy discharges around the house. In addition, she does not need to be confined during oestrus periods or cause the anxiety of unwanted litters at regular intervals.

The neutering of males is less of a benefit to the dog owner, except that it will tend to cut down wandering and some aggression. It is obviously an advantage, if an owner has an unneutered bitch in the household, to have any males neutered if they are not part of the breeding programme

The operation carried out to neuter males is called castration and consists of the surgical removal of the sex organs known as the testes. It is not a particularly effective means of birth control in a population of dogs, as the number of males that would need to be castrated would have to be very large indeed to be effective. On the other hand, every single bitch that is spayed helps much more in keeping the population within reasonable bounds.

It is possible to make a male dog infertile by vasectomy, but the dog will still retain all the

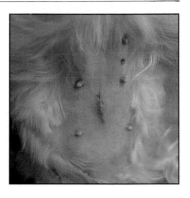

Above: *Small mid-line wounds soon heal after spaying.*

other aspects of sexual behaviour, and these can be eliminated by castration.

Booking the operation
Both neutering operations have to be carried out under effective anaesthesia and so can be performed only by a vet. Each veterinarian has his own ideas about the best time to carry out these procedures, so the subject is best brought up when the first vaccinations are carried out.

The operations should never be considered before protection by vaccination is complete. Nothing else is required except that the animals to be neutered are healthy, and that bitches are neither pregnant or in oestrus. You should book the appointment in reasonable time, however, as the procedure has to be fitted into the working schedule of the practice.

As with all operative surgery, the vet's instructions about withholding food for a strict period before the operation, or any other requirements, must be observed diligently. Most operations of this type allow the animal to go home the next or even the same day.

Just as instructions before operative surgery must be observed, so the importance of guidance afterwards must be recognized and acted upon.

BREEDING AND MATING

Everything should be done to avoid unnecessary breeding of dogs. Unwanted dogs usually lead a miserable life, are often a nuisance and can cause a risk to the public in several different ways. However, breeding from a good dog in a planned way can be useful and rewarding. If there was no breeding, there would be no dogs and our world would be the poorer for that.

The key to success is in the planning. If a good bitch is mated to a dog of known, reliable ancestry this improves the propects of success. You will need to set aside some resources, including your time, especially when caring for the bitch and her litter of puppies.

Anyone who embarks on a breeding programme for their

Below: *A well planned litter can be a joy, but unwanted puppies can be a worry and a burden to everyone concerned.*

bitch as a means of making some money is likely to be disappointed. If all the items are costed properly, the 'amateur' breeder is not likely to be much in funds at the end of it all and may well find, even if all the puppies are sold soon after weaning, that he or she may actually be financially worse off.

The most valid reasons for breeding dogs relate to perpetuating some of the qualities of the parents. As has been emphasized in the last chapter, it is not 'good' for the bitch to have a litter just for the sake of breeding.

Planning a breeding programme
Having decided to breed from a bitch, the next question to be answered is 'when?' Bitches will only accept the male during oestrus periods. These are usually called being 'on heat' and normally last about three weeks. They begin, in average-sized

Above: *Unwanted, stray dogs are both a nuisance and a hazard.*

Above: *Mongrels result from uncontrolled breeding.*

individuals, soon after the bitch is about six months old. This means that the bitch may well be able to be mated and conceive before she is fully mature. Most authorities, however, advise against mating a bitch as early as the first season.

Although there is not much scientific evidence to show that it is actually harmful, it makes sense to prevent a bitch having to rear a litter while she is still growing. With most breeds, waiting until the second season, or when the bitch is about 18 months old at least, is wise. It is not really possible to make any firm judgements on the bitch's qualities before then in any case.

Having decided to begin a breeding programme, the first point to make clear is that the inheritance of physical characteristics is a very complex process indeed. Features present in the parents are not the same as those that will be inherited. Many hidden traits may become evident in the next generation, and features that were hoped for may not appear in the puppies.

In the end, the resulting litter is usually something of a compromise showing much of the appearance of both parents, but with a good sprinkling of features

which make each individual unique. It is easy to fall into the trap of imagining that to become a successful breeder all you need do is to cross two individuals which have all the characteristics thought to be desirable.

Another myth which needs to be put to rest is the idea that mismating will in some way 'taint' a bitch and spoil her for producing pedigree puppies later on. A crossbred litter will have no effect on the quality of subsequent offspring.

Seeking the right mate

The best way to begin to look for a male to mate with a bitch of the same breed is by contacting the breeder of the animal. Not only can the original breeder advise on the most suitable sire, but he or she can probably help to make the arrangements in good time.

Alternatively, the various specialist magazines on dogs, certain directories and even the local press are fruitful sources of information on this subject. Having done this research you can arrange to visit the breeder of the proposed sire and to make some assessment of the dog and, if possible, some of the puppies he has sired. You will get some idea of the general health and the temperament of the dog before you have to make any commitment.

Oestrus

Most bitches come into season or oestrus about every six months. This is more often than not in the spring and autumn, but there is a great deal of variation between individuals.

Below: *The three variations of the oestrous cycle.*

The first oestrus period is often barely noticeable to humans and it is often called the 'silent' heat. All the same, a male or two in the district may notice it very quickly and so it can happen that a bitch is mated before the owner has realized she was even ready.

Later oestrus periods are more obvious. The local swelling of the genital organs, accompanied by discharges which are eventually blood-stained, are easily seen, but it is the change in behaviour that surprises many owners. What was

THE OESTROUS CYCLE OF THE BITCH

Band 1
Normal cycle throughout life
A 10 days. Pro-oestrus. Vulva swelling and bleeding.
B 5 days. Oestrus. Greatest sexual attraction and acceptance of dog.
B1 2–3 days. Ovulation at beginning of oestrus.
C 15 days. Sex attraction wanes.
E 5–7 months. An-oestrus Sexual inactivity.

Band 2
False or Pseudo-pregnancy
A 10 days. Pro-oestrus. Vulva swelling and bleeding.
B 5 days. Oestrus. Greatest sexual attraction and acceptance of dog.
B1 2–3 days. Ovulation.
C 63 days. False pregnancy.
X Imaginary whelping.
D 10 days. Imaginary puppy rearing.
E 4½–5½ months. An-oestrus.

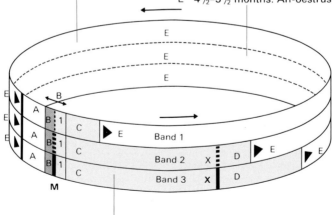

Band 3
True pregnancy
A 10 days. Pro-oestrus. Vulva swelling and bleeding.
B 5 days. Oestrus. Greatest sexual attraction and acceptance of dog.

B1 2–3 days. Ovulation.
M Mating.
C 63 days. Pregnancy.
X Whelping.
D Up to 60 days. Puppy rearing.
E 3½–5½ months. An-oestrus.

a quiet, home-loving and obedient bitch can soon become apparently wanton.

A bitch in oestrus will often actively seek a mate, and break out of the house to satisfy a desire fired by powerful hormones. This often comes as a shock to an owner who thought all the problems would be keeping the canine admirers away.

In the early stages of oestrus, a bitch will be very attractive to males: so much so that they seem to be drawn from all corners and may sit and wait in eager anticipation, or jump the most formidable obstacles, to get at the bitch. Taking a bitch out at this time, even on a lead in great secret, will advertise the fact that she is in oestrus as she will take the scent with her and leave a trail straight back to the house for every dog around.

Although the bitch attracts the dog and may even stand with her tail to one side, she will only accept proper mating in the later stages of oestrus.

Most breeders mate their bitches at least twice, between the eleventh and the fourteenth days of oestrus. The crucial time is indicated by the blood-stained discharge becoming more sticky. This is the most likely time for conception to be achieved, but it must be stressed that a bitch may well be successfully mated up to nearly two weeks after this. It is easy to relax the control measures too soon and have an unwanted litter in the house as a result.

The actual control over the mating is best left to the owner of the stud dog, but the least human interference in the process is usually for the best. It makes sense for an experienced male to be used when the bitch is untried, and *vice versa*.

False pregnancy

Like many other species, bitches prepare themselves for having young whether they conceive or not. A bitch that is not pregnant very often shows all the signs of being about to give birth, without actually doing so. This condition of false pregnancy can be regarded as normality, in the sense that any bitch in the wild state would almost certainly become pregnant, so not being mated whilst in season is the abnormal state.

Some individuals take it to an extreme – even to the point of coming into full lactation (producing milk for puppies), increasing bodyweight and building a 'nest' out of bedding or any other available material.

Owners often become anxious when they see their bitch protecting objects in her nest as if they were puppies. Squeaky toys are greatly favoured, and this can be a source of conflict with any children in the home.

Bitches with false pregnancy can be used as foster mothers when in full lactation, and others may experience quite a lot of discomfort from the accumulated milk, where there are no puppies to suckle. Drawing the milk off by hand is only a temporary help as it simply stimulates the production of more.

Pregnancy

Early pregnancy is in fact quite difficult to distinguish from the false type. The only sure way is to determine that there is a foetus

Above: *The signs of pregnancy are not always very obvious.*

present in the uterus. This is usually established by feeling or, in technical terms, manual palpation of the abdomen. An experienced vet can normally feel a puppy in a cooperative bitch between three and four weeks into pregnancy.

It is much easier to be sure that there is a puppy there, than to be positive that there is not. No chemical tests are yet available for pregnancy testing in bitches, and X-rays are not advised unless there is good reason, and then only in the final stages. Ultrasound equipment is safe and effective, but the cost is still very high and few veterinary practices have this facility as yet.

Normal pregnancy lasts nine weeks, but there is a good deal of variation, and four or five days

Above: *A simple whelping box is quite easily constructed.*

Below: *Embryos in the uterus and their rates of growth.*

EMBRYOS IMPLANTED IN THE UTERUS AT ABOUT 17 DAYS

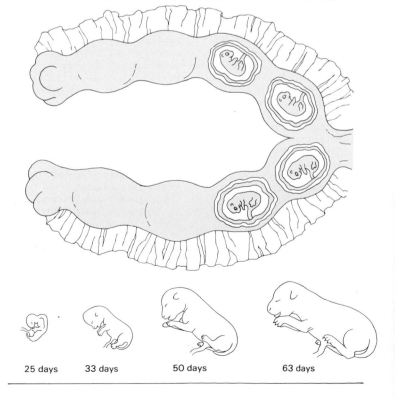

25 days 33 days 50 days 63 days

Above: *Smaller breeds may need privacy during whelping.*

Above: *Bitches need room to turn round and stretch out.*

either way is nothing extraordinary. A bitch will still remain in season for several days after mating, so care has to be taken to avoid additional matings which produce unwanted puppies even if the first mating is successful. This can certainly happen, for it is possible to have puppies from more than one mating present in the same uterus at the same time.

The first six weeks of pregnancy show very little visible change in most bitches, but after this time there is a more dramatic increase in bodyweight, and some enlargement of the teats is seen. Milk can usually be drawn from the teats up to a week before the birth is due. However, these changes can occur in false pregnancy as well and it is easy, even for the experienced, to be deceived.

Preparations for whelping
There is no need to restrict a pregnant bitch's activity, beyond avoiding any great exertion, until the last third of the term. At this time feeding should be increased by 25-30 percent to allow for the rapid acceleration in puppy growth.

If the bitch is already receiving a balanced and wholesome diet,

simply increase the amount of each constituent in the same proportion. It is not necessary (and may be harmful) to give an assortment of vitamin and mineral supplements at this stage in the hope that it will result in bigger and more puppies.

Provide a suitable box in which whelping can take place, and allow the bitch to get used to it and its location for at least three weeks before the birth is due. The box should be located in a reasonably quiet but dry and warm place where you can observe what goes on without disturbance. The box should be large enough for the bitch to turn around in, as well as be able to stretch out to suckle her puppies. It should also have a low front to allow her access.

Line the box with a suitable litter: this can be a few sheets of clean newspaper, which you can change as the need arises, or else a blanket or blankets, which can be washed frequently. Whelping is a messy business, so start collecting a supply of newspaper well in advance, to be sure you have enough to cope when the time comes.

The hair at the bitch's rear should be clipped quite short during the last week.

BIRTH AND GROWING UP

The process of giving birth to a litter of puppies is hard to describe adequately, but an unforgettable event for the family. The first stage of birth is a period of restlessness on the part of the bitch. She will usually start to tear up her bedding and attempt to make a 'nest' for herself, preferably in the whelping box. She will get up and sit down a great deal, and not seem relaxed in either position.

Visible bodily symptoms consist of a general slackening of the tautness of the hind quarters, a slight vaginal discharge and a good deal of swelling of the genital area, in preparation for giving birth.

Below: *Puppies which are delivered in their membranes must have them removed so that they can breathe.*

As an owner, all you need to do at this stage is to make the bitch as comfortable as possible, and to write down the time of every development you notice, as it occurs. This information may well be important if the vet needs to intervene later on. The three main phases of birth to note are: (i) restlessness, (ii) labour or 'contractions' in which the puppies begin to leave their place in the womb, and (iii) delivery itself.

Many bitches vomit shortly before going into labour – this is work that has to be done on an empty stomach. A sure sign of impending labour is a marked drop in body temperature. To observe this, take the bitch's temperature at regular intervals via the rectum, but it is most important to use only a stubby-ended thermometer.

THE BIRTH OF A PUPPY

1 The 'water bag' containing the puppy appears at the vulva

2 The puppy, still encased in the bag, emerges, usually head-first

3 The bitch tears off the bag and gives the puppy a good wash

4 The puppy's head is freed first so that it may take its first breath

Above: *The process of giving birth may take many hours.*

Below: *Newborn puppies must be kept warm and dry.*

If delays occur

If there are no signs of birth beginning, even though the due date has come and gone, normally you need not worry as long as the bitch still looks well, eats and drinks and does not vomit or produce unusual discharges. The first thing to check is your own estimate of the date of delivery: mistakes can easily creep in here, especially if there has been more than one mating.

You do need to call the vet, however, if there is any sign of ill-health, or if more than five days have passed beyond the expected date of birth. The bitch may not be pregnant at all, and this will need to be checked. One sign of the pregnancy is if, during the first phase of birth, the bitch periodically looks round at her flank. If so, when proper straining begins it is important to make a note of the time again.

Labour and delivery

Up to this point most bitches find it reassuring to have people around whom they know, but as the business of having puppies begins in earnest, mothers soon start to resent intrusion. All unnecessary spectators must be excluded from the area: observation without interference

should be the main aim of owners at this stage.

The first positive sign of a puppy is usually the appearance of a small fluid-filled sac which heralds the movement of a puppy down the birth canal. No more than two hours should pass from the start of regular straining until the appearance of a puppy. Allowing for the time it takes for the vet to arrive, in practical terms you should never let a bitch strain in earnest for more than an hour without sending for help.

All being well, with further efforts, a puppy will eventually emerge. It is normally covered with a double layer of membranes, from which it has to be freed to be able to breathe at all. The membranes often rupture where the birth occurs, or if not, the bitch may clear them away.

Above: *The mother–puppy bond should be formed immediately.*

Whatever happens it is vital that anything obstructing the puppy's airway is cleared as soon as possible. A clean, dry towel is adequate for this purpose.

Once the puppy is born it is very important to allow the bitch to see and lick her young. This not only stimulates the puppy into activity, but also helps to create a firm bond between mother and offspring.

If there is a delay during delivery, and the bitch is clearly having difficulty in moving the puppy along, it is quite in order to apply firm but gentle help. This is achieved by wrapping the puppy and its membranes in a clean dry towel, and pulling downwards and backwards. It is not necessary to apply force. If this intervention is unsuccessful, professional help is needed without delay.

Any puppy which seems lifeless and neither moves nor makes any noises should be checked immediately to see if its airway is clear. It should then be rubbed vigorously, but not clumsily, with a dry warm towel. As soon as it makes a healthy sound it should be replaced with its mother. New-born puppies are unable to control their own body temperature, so the environmental temperature must be kept up to around 27-30°C (80-85°F).

Post-natal care

When a bitch has finished whelping, she should be allowed to settle down in the whelping box, and the room kept warm and free from draughts. Make sure the puppies stay with their mother in the box. Infra-red heaters can be used, but take great care to avoid heating the puppies directly: if they are unable to escape the direct beam, this can dry them out rapidly, possibly with fatal consequences.

You may need to coax the mother to come out of the box to relieve herself, as she may be unwilling; but it is very important that she does so, or she may suffer from a bladder illness known as retention cystitis.

It is not at all easy to tell if there are any puppies still to come, so once all the activity is over, it is best to have the mother and litter examined by a vet. As well as checking to see if it is all over, the vet can examine any weakly puppies and give suitable advice. The vet will be able to detect any faults in the puppy that are congenital, i.e. present from birth but not necessarily inherited from the parents, and advise on the best course of action. This is also a very good time to

Left: *Healthy puppies begin to feed within minutes of birth.*

address and telephone number of which can usually be found via the original breeder or by way of the Kennel Club.

Hand rearing

If you do not succeed in finding a foster mother immediately, then the puppies' only chance of survival will be through hand rearing. This is difficult but many find it a rewarding task. Commercial foods are available for this purpose, but you can prepare a formula food yourself.

There is one other vitally important task for the owner in hand rearing, and that is to simulate the action of the mother when she licks the base of each puppy to stimulate it to relieve itself. You have to do this after each feed for at least two weeks, day and night.

This can be achieved by stroking a piece of damp cotton wool over the puppy's rear end. Although the prospect of continual care, day and night for what will seem a very long time,

discuss with the vet any minor cosmetic operations such as removal of the dew claws in some breeds, or even tail docking where this remains a practice.

Occasionally the mother may be unable to suckle her puppies, either through lack of milk or through illness; while sometimes bitches simply seem unwilling to suckle. If this happens, or if the mother should die, you should seek a foster mother without any delay. This is best done through the appropriate breed club, the

BOTTLE-FEEDING

Hold the puppy with its front legs free to 'knead', and the hind legs to stretch and kick.

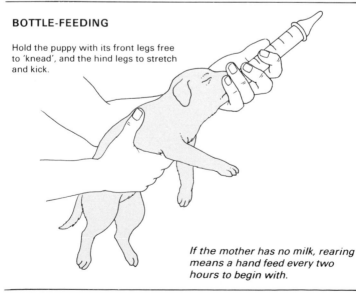

If the mother has no milk, rearing means a hand feed every two hours to begin with.

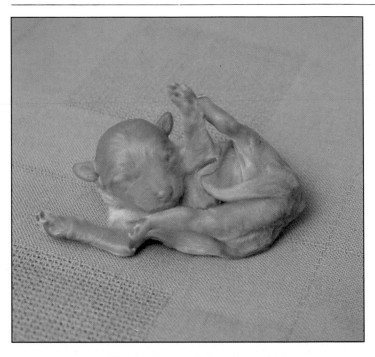

Above: *A righting reflex develops within 3 days.*

Below: *Around 10 days the puppies' eyes are open.*

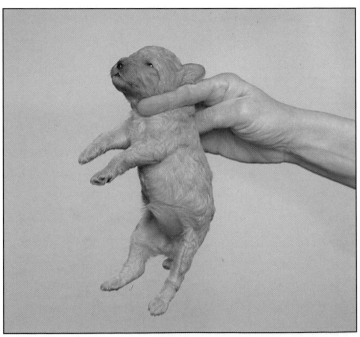

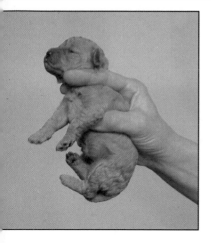

Above: *Flexing muscles predominate up to day 5.*

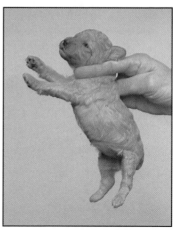

Above: *Extensor muscles predominate from 5–18 days.*

is daunting, the successful rearing of a litter by hand is a considerable achievement and brings with it its own satisfaction.

Each day's feed must be made up fresh and fed at blood heat. It is given to the puppy by hand, by means of a miniature bottle with a rubber teat, or a plastic syringe. A supply of these can usually be obtained from the local veterinary practice.

Suckling and weaning

For bitches who succeed in suckling their own puppies, this is an extremely demanding time. The new-born puppies are entirely dependent on her milk for the first three weeks or so of their lives. They must be left undisturbed while they feed, which they will do day and night until they are capable of eating some solid food.

The presence of any humans at feeding time will reduce the amount of nourishment they get. It is crucial that the temptation to show off the litter to friends is resisted at least until the puppies can take some solid food.

Puppies start to eat solid food, usually by discovering what their mother is eating, at about the time they begin to explore.

Development of puppies

Puppies are all born with only the basic senses of touch, taste and smell. They feel cold and warmth as well as pain and hunger. They cannot see or hear very much until their eyes have been open for a day or so. This begins to happen at about the tenth day. But it is some two and a half to three weeks before they actively start to explore their surroundings.

The progression of characteristic behavioural skills that the young puppy develops follows a fairly fixed sequence, and it is extremely important that the process of socialization takes place in as normal a way as possible during this time. The first thing a puppy has to learn is that it is a pack animal and that it is a dog. So it needs to mix with others of its species. It then has to be aware of other species that are not dogs, and learn where it and they fit in.

It makes good practical sense to allow puppies to become accustomed to other species kept as pet animals, such as cats and rabbits or even rats and mice, at an early age, so that they can all live in harmony together.

Puppies reared in isolation,

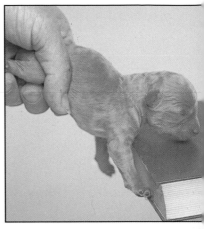

Above: *At birth, the puppy only passes urine by a reflex stimulation by mother or hand.*

Above: *Up until 5 days, the puppy's limb placing reflexes are completely undeveloped.*

without seeing any dogs other than their mother at birth, and no more than one or two humans from then on, are prone to develop behavioural problems later in life.

Main phases
Here is a list of the main phases of puppy development. Time periods for this development are not fixed, and vary slightly between individuals as in any natural process.

At birth. Puppies' eyes remain closed, and the puppies have no sense of hearing or smell. They feel pain, heat, cold, hunger and thirst. They are asleep for at least nine tenths of the time and spend the rest seeking food from their mother. They pull themselves along with a 'swimming' action. They cannot walk or even stand up. The sucking reflex is very strong. They need their mother to stimulate urination and defaecation by licking their hindquarters.

At around ten days. The eyes open but it takes one to two weeks more for the puppies to develop fully acute vision.

From two to three weeks. The senses of hearing and smell start to function. The puppy is now able to walk with quite a lot of control. It develops the ability to relieve itself at will, independently of its mother. It begins to learn from experience and to avoid things that it has found to be unpleasant. As it begins to explore its surroundings, the puppy will eat anything that looks at all like food. This often happens as a result of walking through food put down for the mother.

From three to four weeks. The puppy emerges from its earliest infancy and is ready to undertake the period of socialization. Through interaction with its mother and litter-mates, it forms an intricate and varied set of behaviour patterns, which remain intact for the rest of its life. The puppy now weighs some six or seven times its birth weight.

From eight to ten weeks. The amount of milk the puppy takes, or is allowed to take, from its mother, diminishes rapidly. After the period of socializing with dogs and other pets, comes the time

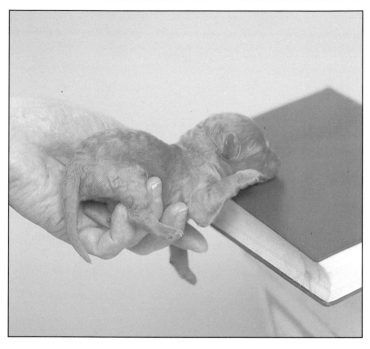

Above: *A fore-limb placing reflex develops from day 5.*

Below: *The hind-limb placing reflex is evident from day 12.*

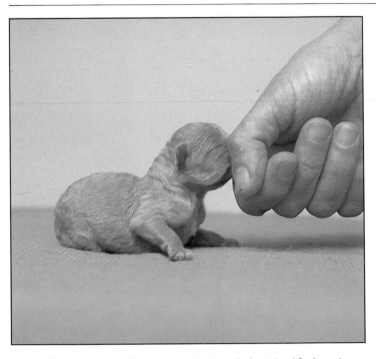

Above: *The 'rooting' reflex is strong in the puppy by day 12.*

Below: *Before day 10, there is no eyesight and little hearing.*

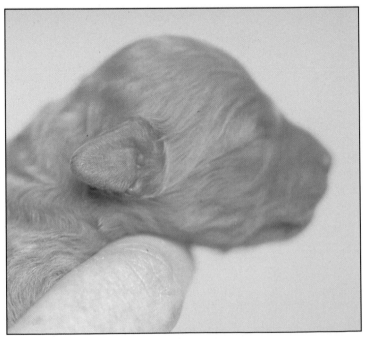

Above: *After day 10 there is more awareness of the environment.*

for socialization with humans. If the puppy is deprived of all human contact it will almost certainly be impossible for it to adapt to human living conditions, and it will probably be completely uncontrollable. It learns from its mother how to fit into both canine and human society.

Leaving the litter. Most puppies that are sold to pet owners are taken into their new and permanent homes at around eight weeks, but there are many advantages in waiting until as late as 12 or 13 weeks, so that the new puppy is as fully equipped for life as it can be. It also helps to overcome the conflict of interests when the puppy needs to socialize with other dogs, but is not allowed outside because its vaccination programme is not completed and it would therefore be at risk from infection.

When it enters its permanent home, the young dog's position in the hierarchy of the household has to be established. It is of the greatest importance that the human master or mistress is established as the pack leader. If not, the dog may well dominate the whole household and make everyone in it lead a life of misery. Properly integrated into the home, almost all dogs become an asset to their owners' lives.

Below: *The correct way to carry a puppy a few weeks old.*

GAMES FOR DOGS TO PLAY

Play in our dogs pleases the eye and warms the soul, but why do they do it? It would seem to be an unusual example of animals doing something for no substantial outcome.

Play is a special feature of animals which live in complex and organized groups – like man himself; like the wolf and its derivative the dog. This gives a clue to the function of play: the development of language, and the exchange of signals with others in the group. Play for dogs is a high-speed emotional acitivity that confuses threat with appeasement, sexual advance with rejection, food-begging with object procurement and so on.

Play is often so fast that slow-speed video replay is an essential tool for effective observation. This

Below: *Group play can reveal the complex society of dogs.*

has shown that skills needed for hunting, social competition for rank order, courtship, sexual success and care of young all have their roots in play.

Play through the years
Puppies begin to play when they are about three weeks old, usually in badly-coordinated mouthing of the heads of litter-mates. By four weeks, definite play postures involving the whole body present the signal 'What now follows is play and should not be taken too seriously'.

With sharp milk teeth, nips from a month-old puppy can be quite painful, so the protective wince and snap from the mother or other 'victim' of rough play soon teaches the skill of bite-inhibition. Puppies learn the consequences of their biting, and to maintain gentle play owners should not rough-house whilst

wearing gloves. They need the feedback of pained yelps to educate inhibited mouthing.

By five weeks, play between puppies can become quite aggressive and more precise as the central nervous system matures. Definite adult facial expressions take over from the more rounded mask of the puppy. Sex appears on the scene by six weeks of age, especially amongst male puppies. The importance of this learning phase has been demonstrated experimentally: lonely puppies deprived of the opportunity to play make poor mates as adults.

The duration of play amongst puppies declines noticeably after 10 weeks of age; but as any dog owner knows, play continues for life and into the twilight years. It is performed whenever inclination coincides with invitation.

Above: *Dominance and submission are two vital signals.*

Above: *By week 3, puppies begin to play-mouth litter-mates.*

Above: *Play in older puppies can become quite aggressive as their nervous systems develop.*

67

Right: *One of the most important forms of canine play is hide and seek, in which the dog exercises all its skills in finding its human partner.*

No scientific data are available on whether or not some breeds of dogs are more playful than others, but it is my experience that heavier-bodied breeds like Mastiffs, St Bernards or Labradors are less skittish than a tireless Terrier or silly Setter. These differences can be accounted for by the variations in body weight. Slim a Labrador or fatten a Setter, and play will increase or decrease accordingly.

Adult male dogs tend to be more playful than bitches, again possibly explained by the higher fat levels on the female form. A slim, healthy bitch can be as playful as any dog, though the type of play will differ between the sexes. A typical sequence of play for dogs of either sex might begin with a bow, followed by a growling bark, an exaggerated approach, veering to one side, a chase, mouth-muzzle biting, rolling-wrestling, more chasing, more wrestling, knocking over, standing astride, rearing, pushing and pulling. Pure joy!

Games you can play
Dogs can be broadly classified as either plodders or pushers, tendencies which can be guided by the owner, so don't let your dog be bored and boring: start playing!

Hide and seek This game has important survival implications for wild dogs: separation from the pack means loss of protection and possibly being eaten. All the senses are stretched in hide and seek: to smell disturbed earth, crushed grass and body odours; to hear the slightest sound, or see movement.

Amongst dogs the successful find of the hiding partner ends with a pounce or ambush. Since

Above: *The play bow is one of the moves by which play begins.*

the reward for finding is in the pounce, human partners of hide and seek games should try to do the same. Don't be inhibited.

The game has many variations but start by running behind a tree

Above: *Holding and mouthing objects is a favourite game.*

Above: *Play can involve such athletic moves as rearing.*

or wall, then encourage the following. Make the distance travelled greater, and have some one else hold the canine partner back to give you a headstart. Later and after six months of age, teach 'sit' or 'down' and 'stay' as a preliminary to the 'find' invitation.

The final phase of difficulty in this game is to move in the third dimension: climb a tree or drop into a hole for instance.

Above: *One of the first stages in teaching 'seek and find'.*

Below: *Praise and play should reward a lesson well-learnt.*

Object seek and find The sense of smell in pet dogs is rarely challenged or worked as much as it is in their wild relatives. It is easy to teach most dogs the habit of searching or scent-trailing. Springer Spaniels and Labradors making impressive drug-finds from suitcases at airports are no different from other dogs with enthusiasm and a desire to please their owners.

Returning must always be rewarded by fuss and uninhibited

fun. Take a favourite toy and show the dog that you are placing it under a carpet. Lift the carpet, drop, lift and so on until the object is seen and grabbed.

Once the idea of an object being available but not visible is established, the sense of smell will be called into action. Make the 'hides' more complex so that the dog can't see where the object is being placed.

Keep the objects or scents to be found simple or few in number:

Above: *Scent-trailing can turn into quite a sport for some.*

Below: *Taught early, most dogs can learn to play 'retrieve'.*

socks, cheese or a characteristically scented dumbell for instance. Specialist trainers use a hollow metal tube punched with holes, through which the search aroma can escape.

As skill and enthusiasm of a dog finding a particular odour improves, one need place less of the substance in the tube. For instance, a non-smoker could teach his or her dog to find cigarettes, and quite soon a single shred of tobacco leaf should be detected.

Dogs can also be trained to trail after people or animals in true Bloodhound fashion. Specialist clubs exist where members and their dogs develop their skill of scent-trailing. It is highly recommended as a healthy, outdoor pursuit, be you the pursuing or the pursued!

Retrieve The tendency to carry and retrieve objects is to a great extent genetically determined: Golden Retrievers and Spaniels obviously have it, and most Terriers do not. The tendency to hold objects in the mouth can,

however, be encouraged in puppies by pretend efforts to repossess, with a 'give it to me!' tone of voice. Once this holding tendency has formed in the puppy, it can be easily linked to the 'come' and 'drop' commands.

After initial puppy training, it is very important to insist on the dog returning with the object to you, and not chase after the dog in a catch game. Stand still, wait and don't begin to praise until the object is actually in your hands.

Below: *Safe toys should be chewable but not destructible!*

Above: *Safe play objects like this canvas dumbbell are best.*

A word of caution on the use of sticks as play objects. They can be quite dangerous by leaving splinters between the teeth or penetrating the gums. Never throw sticks as dogs can run into them with terrible consequences to the throat. Rubber rings, large balls and hessian or canvas dumbbells are safer. Squeaky toys should be of the latex kind. They last longer and are safer than vinyl.

Tag This game of catch-me-if-you-can comes easily to dogs, and keeps everybody fit.

Water Most dogs will swim if they have to, but many don't appreciate the potential for

buoyant goonery which water offers. It is all a matter of introducing puppies to water early: teach them to swim as one does a child, by example.

Word and song The vocal repertoire of dogs is really quite extensive and an observant trainer can encourage a particular type of bark. Thus, dogs can apparently 'speak' on command. The tendency to howl is particularly strong in some individuals, giving the potential for conducting melodic renditions of favourite songs.

My younger Irish Setter Sam varies the pitch and intensity of his howling precisely to follow the human accompanist's voice and hand position.

Sport The competitive spirit in man is often expressed through our dogs, which may or may not be to their advantage. However, the sport of agility-trialing is particularly recommended because it is as exhausting for the human as for the dog, and hilarious for spectators.

Unfortunately, some participants of canine agility take it far too seriously and try to complete the obstacle course

Above: *Many dogs do not make the most out of water play.*

Below: *But many dogs need no excuse to enjoy water.*

faster than anyone else. Thus the dominance of speedy Border Collies in this sport! Agility trialing between Bassets or Basenjis is just as much fun.

In the dog we humans have chosen an intelligent, social animal as a companion. It is not enough that we feed, warm and walk our dogs. They also need our time, love and fun. Playing with dogs does us a power of good!

73

YOUR DOG'S HEALTH

Ailments and symptoms
Assuming a dog is protected by vaccination (see the relevant chapter and Table 5), this chapter aims to help owners to deal with the situation when a dog becomes ill. It will not be organized in the way that ailments' sections are traditionally done in dog books and simply list the diseases from A to Z. This would assume that the reader already knows the symptoms or signs of the disease, which cannot be expected.

Instead, the majority of entries will approach the problem from **what the owner sees** (the clinical signs). The chapter will next move on via what the dog feels or seems to be feeling (the symptoms) to some likely diagnoses of the illnesses and to possible courses of action.

Some courses of action count as first aid and are therefore referred to in Emergency Care.

Digestive system
Abdominal pain The pain may be felt in a different place from the actual site of the problem: this is known as 'referred pain'. In mild abdominal pain the dog resents being handled anywhere in the hind part of the body. In severe cases it may collapse or remain rigid (see Emergency Care).

Very severe pain just behind the stomach may be caused by acute inflammation of the pancreas. A sign of this is 'praying' – the dog stands with hindquarters raised and forelegs lowered, in an attempt to relieve the pain it is experiencing.

In all cases of abdominal pain withhold food, give fluids only and take to the veterinarian.

Appetite loss (i) Complete lack of appetite (anorexia), is acceptable for one day. If it continues to a second day then veterinary attention is needed.

(ii) Call the veterinary practice, too, if the dog clearly wants to eat but is physically unable to, or shows signs of pain whenever it tries.

(iii) Inappetence, on the other hand, is not a complete failure to eat but simply a poor appetite. This can simply be the result of overfeeding, but it may be a symptom of illness. If, for example, the dog shows signs of **fever** (listlessness, persistent panting, lying down) contact the veterinarian.

Less obvious causes of inappetence are behavioural problems. A dog may experience serious stress in its relationships within the household. Behavioural therapy may be the solution: it is a specialized branch of veterinary work which may, for example, involve investigating all activities within the family, with a view to altering the status of some members, human or dog.

Overeating (i) Some dog breeds are notoriously greedy – especially hounds and some gun dogs. Prevention by careful control of meals is much easier than trying to reverse the state.

TABLE 5: THE DISEASES WHICH THE DOG CAN BE PROTECTED AGAINST BY VACCINATION

Canine Distemper (CDV)
Canine Viral Hepatitis (CVH)
Canine Parvovirus Disease (CPV)
Rabies (Only in countries where rabies is present)
Kennel Cough (against some of the organisms involved)
Leptospirosis (against some of the organisms involved)

DIGESTIVE SYSTEM OF THE DOG

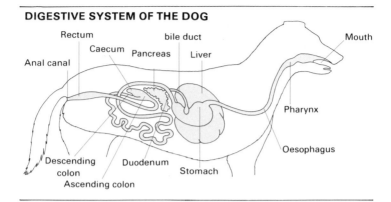

Above: *Dogs have quite a short digestive system, but it is a very efficient one.*

(ii) Overeating by a dog that remains underweight may be a problem of poor absorption, in which case adjusting the diet may help.

(iii) Continual loss of weight while eating normally, especially with an increase in thirst, may be a sign of **diabetes mellitus**. This is a disorder of the carbohydrate metabolism which requires emergency treatment (diabetes can be fatal) and long-term management often involving daily injections of insulin. Another possibility is a **tumour**, which requires specialist veterinary advice.

Depraved appetite (i) Discourage dogs from eating carrion, if only on the grounds of avoiding infection.

(ii) Eating grass (in small amounts) comes naturally to dogs, and although owners are sometimes distressed to see the dog vomit afterwards, this is the normal and healthy purpose of the exercise.

(iii) Eating earth or clay, or large quantities of grass, is a sign of serious disorder, possibly behavioural in nature (see page 74).

(iv) Eating faeces is called coprophagia and is usually much more upsetting for the owners than for the dogs. Causes are usually behavioural, or simply boredom in dogs that lack companionship or are continually kennelled. To train the dog off the habit you can use the command 'No!' in good time; distract it with games (within reason); make faeces repugnant by adding mustard, pepper or tabasco powder; and lead the dog briskly away. But the best hope lies in prevention or behavioural analysis and treatment.

Diarrhoea Most cases result from eating garbage, gross overeating or sudden changes in diet. Most are self-limiting (they clear up without treatment).

Urgent veterinary help is needed if diarrhoea is persistent, especially when accompanied by vomiting; if blood is clearly visible or the faeces are very dark, indicating blood; or if faeces are putty-coloured and foul-smelling, indicating poor digestion by the dog of fats.

If you see signs of parasites (usually as whole worms but sometimes other forms as small white segments like rice) this is not an emergency, but obtain anti-worm treatment from a veterinary practice as soon as you can.

To treat diarrhoea, it is normal to withhold liver and milk, because some dogs are not able

75

to digest them well. It may be necessary to investigate the possibility of some other cause of a digestive reaction.

Withhold solid food altogether for the first 24 hours, offering glucose and water, plus a fluid suspension of a very digestible food (such as canned puppy food made up into a mousse). Then gradually return to the normal diet, if all goes well, over one or two days.

Gastric dilation and torsion ('bloat') Clinical signs: unsuccessful attempts to vomit; collapse; death if not treated immediately. This is one of the situations where a few minutes can make the difference between life and death. Telephone the local veterinarian or even set off at once if there is someone else who can telephone while you are on the way.

The illness consists of a sudden accumulation of gas in the stomach, which has rotated about its horizontal axis so as to twist tight the exit points. Pressure from the swelling stomach restricts the flow of blood to the vital organs, and may interfere with the heart's function.

There is very little you can do by way of first aid. The vet may relieve the gas and correct the torsion surgically: take advice on aftercare. See Emergency Care.

Foreign body in the mouth or throat Signs: excessive salivation, reluctance to eat, obvious pain on attempting to eat, pawing at the mouth; choking, in which case the dog may collapse and the inside of the mouth go blue.

Action: remove any obvious items; if the inside of the mouth has gone blue this is an extreme emergency and you must try to feel inside the throat in case you can clear the obstacle. Use the handle of a spoon rather than anything pointed. An emergency call to the veterinary practice may be necessary to remove it.

DOG WORMS WITH EGGS
(Not to scale)

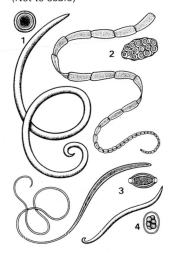

1 Roundworm **2** Tapeworm
3 Whipworm **4** Hookworm
Antiworm treatment should be given for round and tapeworms

Foreign body in the gut Small stones, pebbles and rubber balls can get stuck in the gut, though very often the dog will successfully pass these. Veterinary surveillance is essential. Do not feed until the veterinarian gives the go-ahead.

Vomiting Most dogs vomit readily, often without discomfort. To us this is repulsive, but it serves the dog's health well by clearing the stomach of unwanted material although many re-eat what they have brought up. Vomiting is a natural part of canine behaviour, and bitches have the ability to regurgitate partly digested food for their puppies at weaning.

Persistent vomiting, however, should be reported to the vet. If accompanied by diarrhoea, it soon leads to dehydration; give small amounts of drinking water with some glucose and get the dog examined by a veterinarian as soon as possible.

Constipation A common cause is sudden introduction of bones to the diet, when the dog is not used to them. The vet may give an enema to clear the dog's rectum.

Ageing dogs may lose some motility of their gut, causing constipation; feed these with some bran in the food or give a gel laxative. Old male dogs may become constipated because of an enlargement of the prostate gland which begins to press on the gut. This usually requires hormone treatment.

Respiratory system
Discharge from the nose Small amounts of clear discharge are not abnormal, but profuse amounts are.

Seek urgent veterinary help if: (i) the discharge is not clear but dark, (ii) it contains pus, (iii) it does not cease within, say, an hour, (iv) it obviously causes the dog pain, (v) it contains blood, (vi) it is accompanied with a similar flow from the eyes or (vii) the dog is simultaneously showing other symptoms of illness.

Dry, crusty nose This can be a sign of **canine distemper** (page 46). More often, it is a sign of ageing: look to see if the skin is thickening elsewhere, such as on the pads or the ear tips.

Laboured breathing Normal panting after exertion should subside within a few minutes. If panting continues without any exertion, contact the vet – the dog is likely to be in pain or distress.

Coughing There may be inflammation in the larynx (laryngitis), the windpipe (tracheitis), the bronchial tubes (bronchitis) or the chest wall and lung coverings (pneumonia; pleurisy). Persistent coughing might also be a sign of circulatory congestion (see **Circulation system**, below), canine distemper or, if harsh, kennel cough (see page 46 for details).

Circulatory system
The heart drives a circulation of blood and other fluids around the body, and sends oxygen-depleted blood to the lungs for replenishment. If oxygen-rich blood does not arrive at all tissues continuously, they will die rapidly.

Severe loss of blood (see Emergency Care).

Congestive heart failure
Deterioration of the heart valves (usually with age) or, in rarer cases, disease in the heart muscles, can lead to the heart becoming so inefficient that it cannot propel fluids round the system.

This causes congestion (blood cannot pass along the vessels) and fluid stasis, or the stagnation of body fluids in various possible places. The dog will certainly be weakened and may collapse.

The signs of circulatory congestion in the chest are laboured breathing and a cough that gradually gets worse. Signs of wider circulatory congestion include: the inside of the mouth turning blue; and a pot-bellied appearance (congestion in the abdomen).

Treatment for collapse: see Emergency Care.

Bruises, blood blisters and haematomata These are three names for degrees of the same thing: when a small blood vessel bursts near the skin, some blood accumulates locally and causes a swelling. If it looks particularly dark or bloody, people tend to call it a blood blister.

A large swelling of this kind is called a **haematoma**. If this forms in the ear, the dog may shake its head and cause further damage to its ear. This must be treated by a veterinarian.

Skin and hair
Many skin conditions are slow to resolve, and so patience and perseverance may be needed to

get the skin back to normal. Signs of skin disease are: inflammation; irritation; hair shedding; skin damage; discoloration and thickening.

A dog may show signs of intense irritation when no sign of inflammation can be seen; or it may have very conspicuous inflammation that does not seem to bother it at all; but either case may alter quickly if nothing is done by way of treatment.

Inflammation of the skin The skin reddens, is often swollen and may feel warmer than surrounding areas. The dog shows signs of tenderness and local inflammation. There may be a clear discharge, becoming more opaque as the infection develops and then giving off pus and a bad smell when infected. It may be necessary to clip away hair and clean the area, using warm water only in the vicinity.

Discoloration and thickening of the skin This is a natural consequence of ageing, but it can be a sign of parasites or nutritional disorder.

Treatment: (i) bathing to improve the coat; (ii) extra dietary fat such as corn oil, given two or three times a week, a teaspoonful for a spaniel-sized dog. Ask your veterinarian if a zinc supplement is appropriate.

Skin inflammation inside the ear This is the most frequent problem reported to veterinary practices that deal with pets. Almost as common as primary ear conditions are cases that have been made worse by 'do-it-yourself' treatment at home. The dog's ear is a delicate structure and treating its interior is no task for the amateur.

Fleas and lice These parasites can cause inflammation of the skin. You may see the fleas or their droppings, which are like

Below: *Regular attention is needed for these parasites.*

COMMON DOG PARASITES

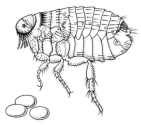

Dog flea (*Ctenocephalides canis*)

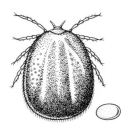

Dog louse (*Linognathus setosus*)

Dog tick (*Ixodes ricinus*)

Follicular mite (*Demodex canis*)

small flecks of soot, often around the head and along the back. Kill fleas and lice by means of suitable baths and dressings; but remember that they lay their eggs away from the dog, so disinfect the dog's whole environment.

Mites The only mites large enough to be readily seen are harvest mites of the genus Trombicula, which appear as little orange specks in some localities. These cause irritation and inflammation around the feet of dogs that spend a lot of time on farmers' fields in summer. Medicated baths are needed.

Other mites are too small to see without magnification. **Demodectic mange** is an upsurge of mites that are present in the skin in small numbers all the time in most dogs. **Sarcoptic mange** is due to invasive mites and is usually the more irritating of the two, as well as being rapidly transferred to other dogs and even to people.

Impaction and inflammation of the anal sacs There are two anal sacs, one each side of the anus. These produce a thick, strongly scented fluid that plays an important part in the signalling system between dogs.

The sacs often become impacted (overfull and irritating); the most obvious sign is that the dog begins to pay a lot of

Above: *Anal sac impaction is the usual reason for scooting.*

attention to its rear end and 'scoot' along on its bottom in an effort to evacuate the sacs. Leave the treatment to the veterinarian.

The itch-scratch cycle
Scratching a place that itches may give temporary relief, but may also increase local inflammation. Dogs often cause self-inflicted damage in this way, and the new wound they have given themselves will itch, so the cycle begins anew.

Causes may be parasites, sand, the spikes of grass seeds (awns), household disinfectants or possibly chemicals in the home, garden or countryside.

Treatment ought to be aimed at removing the original cause of irritation; but palliative treatment (getting rid of the symptoms) is acceptable if it allows the natural healing process to work without further scratching.

Allergic reactions of the skin
These are not common in dogs, but can be caused by sensitivity to certain food components and some substances in the dog's environment. The dog's head may swell up within minutes, and a 'nettle rash' may appear and then quickly recede. Other signs are sudden diarrhoea and bare patches of skin.

Treatment: sophisticated veterinary detective work for proper diagnosis first, including test feeding and possibly a period in hospital; once the substance to which the dog is sensitive is identified, avoid it for good.

Injuries of the skin Bites and cuts are fairly common but for every one you see there may be others hidden under the fur, so look carefully, if necessary cutting the fur back. Besides bites from other animals, common causes include pieces of grit, slivers of glass and carelessly discarded fishing equipment.

Treatment: this is a fairly urgent matter; bites almost

always introduce infection, and cuts are nearly as dangerous. The vet will clean away debris, sew up some wounds (some are best left open), dress them and give appropriate injections.

'Cysts' between the toes These are not cysts but small abscesses. They are seen fairly often in certain breeds, particularly small terriers, such as the West Highland White.

Treatment: clean up the area and apply frequent hot compresses; but they are usually a sign of general debility, so get the dog examined and take appropriate advice.

Hair shedding All dogs except poodles and their close relatives shed some hair continuously. It is normal to moult quite heavily, mainly in spring and autumn, and then to grow new hair. Central heating has reduced the effects of the seasons on this process in many dogs, so their moulting can be less affected by the seasons.

Bad cases of hair loss do occur, however, and these may be signs of a hormonal or nutritional disorder.

Treatment: regular baths in a suitable shampoo will get out the dead hair, and corn oil or zinc supplement in the diet will help nutrition-related cases. If these treatments plus regular grooming do not resolve the problem, see a veterinarian.

Nervous system and senses All the dog's visible activity, and most of what goes on internally, are controlled by nerves. Much of the activity is outside voluntary control: for example, the functioning of the heart, gut and bladder. The effectiveness of treating disorders of such a complex and delicate system is necessarily limited, but the earlier the situation is attended to by a veterinarian, the better the chances of successful treatment and recovery.

Blindness and distorted vision It is not always obvious if a dog is going blind, particularly if it really knows its way around, as dogs can adapt gradually and with great skill to failing eyesight.

Causes can be: (i) deterioration of nervous transmission to the brain, as often happens in very old age; (ii) failure of part of the eye itself – eyelids, cornea, lens, chambers of the eye or retina. Treatment is more likely to be feasible in (ii) than in (i). Eyes should be tested at each annual check-up.

If **vision is distorted** because the lens has become displaced within the eye, or because of a cataract or damage to the cornea, the dog will see objects in places where they are not. This can be treated if detected early.

Deafness This, again, may not be obvious, for the dog may detect a sound by the air disturbance, i.e. using its sense of touch. Also, the ability to hear may wax and wane from day to day at the onset of deafness.

Treatment: the vet will usually be able to treat the ear for (i) obstruction of sound; (ii) damage to the eardrum; (iii) some forms of disturbance to the inner and middle ear (beyond the eardrum).

Loss of smell and taste These senses deteriorate with age and can be seriously impaired during many infectious diseases. Treatment involves clearing the nasal chambers and in dealing with any infection present. If the dog loses appetite, offer it foods warmed and with a stronger, more attractive smell.

Paralysis (see Emergency Care).
Fits (convulsions) These can be very alarming for an owner to see. The only good thing about them is that the dog is probably unaware of what is happening during a fit. The causes are often very hard to establish.

The dog goes very rigid in a

spasm, with limbs and body stretched out. This is followed by a period of intense involuntary activity: legs paddle as if swimming. Occasionally there may be just one fit, but more usually there will be a series of them, and sometimes they come in repeated cycles with intervals of some weeks.

Treatment: if the dog vomits, clear the mouth and throat to prevent suffocation. Put the dog in a quiet place, preferably in a darkened room. Telephone the veterinary practice to ask advice but do not ask for an emergency visit: the fit will probably be over on arrival. Do not rush the dog to the surgery either: avoid all disturbance.

Twitching or excessive shivering
This is known as chorea and, along with many fits, is often an after-effect of **canine distemper** (page 46). It consists of localized, but sometimes severe, twitching of groups of muscles just under the skin, often near the side of the head. Ask the veterinary practice for advice on this as soon as possible.

The twitching seen during normal sleep when dogs are said to be 'dreaming' is not an abnormality.

Reproductive system
Of all the systems covered in this chapter, this is the one that pet dogs can manage without (see page 48). A neutered dog is easier to manage besides having a better chance of a longer life.

False pregnancy (see page 53).

Misalliance Bitches often get mated against the wishes of their owner. Many owners do not realize that a well behaved, obedient bitch may change completely when in oestrus. If she disappears for even a few minutes, she is very likely to have been mated, although the owner may not have seen anything

happening to her.

Treatment: a vet can prevent conception within 36 hours by means of a hormone injection, but the bitch must be in full health. It is not advisable to repeat the injection if misalliance happens again within the same oestrus period.

Abortion Spontaneous abortion is not common in bitches, but it can happen. The owner may see the incompletely formed puppies when aborted, or may simply observe a sudden loss of body weight well before the expected term. Other signs are an unpleasant-looking discharge from the vulva, or she may spend much time licking at her rear end. She may be ill in other ways, and show signs of fever.

These signs are a clear indication that a veterinary examination is needed, if only to check if there is anything that still needs to be evacuated from the uterus – or even if the puppies are premature at all. It is easy to get the dates of mating wrong.

Discharges of pus from genital opening With or without blood, this is always a serious sign, even if it appears to be only temporary. In males it can be due to an infection anywhere in the genital tract. In females the same applies, plus the possibility of a condition known as **pyometra** (pus in the uterus).

Pyometra results from degeneration of the inside of the uterus and usually occurs as part of the process of ageing. The usual solution is to remove the uterus and ovaries surgically.

Oversexed If a bitch remains more or less in permanent oestrus or a male continually mounts everything around, whether it is living or not, then help is needed. It is very likely that something can be done, by chemical or behavioural therapy or simply by neutering the animal.

THE SKELETAL SYSTEM OF THE DOG

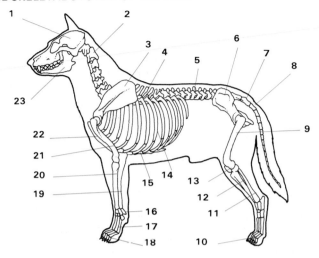

1 Skull	**9** Femur	**17** Metacarpals
2 Neck vertebrae	**10** Hind digits	**18** Front digits
3 Scapula	**11** Fibula	**19** Ulna
4 Thoracic vertebrae	**12** Tibia	**20** Radius
5 Lumbar vertebrae	**13** Patella	**21** Humerus
6 Pelvis	**14** Ribs	**22** Prosternum
7 Sacrum	**15** Sternum	**23** Mandible
8 Coccygeal vertebrae	**16** Carpus	(lower jaw)

Musculo-skeletal system

A dog's body moves under the power of its muscles. Each muscle is attached to a particular point on the dog's skeleton.

The main disorders of the muscles and bones that an owner will see relate to (i) deformities of the bone from faulty development or physical injury; (ii) tenderness due to inflammation; (iii) reduction in muscle size due to wastage and, in a few cases, (iv) growths developing in the bone or muscle structures themselves.

Lameness (i) A dog may be unable to move its limbs properly or it may show signs of pain if it tries. If the dog has been seen twisting or injuring a limb, rest it for a day. If there is no improvement, seek veterinary advice. It is very difficult for an owner to tell exactly why a dog is

Above: *A generalized diagram of the dog skeleton.*

lame, and determining the site of pain is best left to the veterinarian.

(ii) If there is any obvious pain even when there is no movement, then call the vet without delay.

(iii) Persistent lameness due to conditions such as **Hip Dysplasia** (HD) and **osteo-arthritis** can only be diagnosed by a vet.

Back and neck pain The dog may have slipped or dislocated one of the discs between its spinal vertebrae. It may be in acute pain and need veterinary advice.

Swelling in muscle and bone These may simply be bruises, especially if they seem to have appeared suddenly. On the other hand, they may be **tumours** in the

Above: *Excessive thirst may be a symptom of urinary disorder and a sign to seek advice.*

muscle or bone. As these usually grow slowly, they may be difficult to recognize at first and may cause very little inconvenience to begin with.

Always be on the lookout for such swellings. Although bone tumours are very serious, effective treatment is possible.

Urinary system

This consists of the kidneys, urinary bladder and the connecting structures which link them (the ureters) plus the connecting link between the bladder and the outside world, the urethra.

It is only the position where the urethra emerges which differs in the urinary systems of males and females. In the bitch the urinary tract opens into the vulva and in males the urethra passes down the penis through a bone in this structure, the *os penis*.

Increased urine output and thirst

Dogs with urinary disorders usually produce a lot of very dilute urine, with a great increase in their thirst to compensate.

(i) This may be accompanied by some pain, and if pain increases to the point where the dog cannot pass urine at all, get help quickly.

(ii) In cases where the dog can still urinate, there will be loss of fluid, and an increase in thirst to compensate. There may also be a tendency to vomit; this will result in a further loss of fluid, which will have to be made up.

(iii) If **kidney failure** is responsible, the dog's whole condition deteriorates. It becomes 'toxic' because it cannot eliminate some of the waste products from its body, having lost some or all kidney function. Special feeding may help to control the symptoms.

Blood in the urine (i) If the urine is discoloured or has blood in it, the dog needs attention. Inflammation of the bladder (cystitis) is quite common, especially in bitches, as a result of an ascending infection entering the urethra at the vulva.

(ii) The inflammation may also be due to **'bladder stones'** or calculi, which have come out of solution in the urine. These can cause a great deal of discomfort. Effective treatments are available, and surgical removal is normally effective in the short term.

Prevention is directed towards the maintenance of acidity in the urine, a high water turnover so there is no static fluid in the urinary tract, and careful feeding to restrict the materials which go to form urinary stones.

Incontinence Any dog which has little or no control over passing urine must be examined properly to establish the reason. Apart from disorders of the urinary system, as above, there are at least three other possible causes:

(i) behavioural problems – for example, a dog may develop an over-submissive attitude and this may cause it to urinate every time the owner, or even another dog in the household, approaches it. Behavioural therapy is a possible solution (see page 74).

(ii) Pyometra (see under Discharges on page 81); and

(iii) Diabetes mellitus (see reference on page 75).

83

USING YOUR VET

Your veterinary surgeon is there to help you and your animals. You do not need an appointment and a consultation to find out the best time to neuter a dog or what to do about worming. A telephone call or a quick talk with the receptionist or a nurse will do for that.

It is up to you at the outset to visit local veterinary practices and choose the one that you respect and is convenient for you (not just the cheapest). Then keep in touch so that they know you and your dog, and vice versa.

If you just use your local veterinarian for what are called 'fire fighting' jobs such as sudden illness, accidents and emergencies, you are not doing the best for your dog. The work of the veterinary practice should involve total care, from the time an owner first acquires an animal to the last moments of its life.

You will be astonished to find out just how much the average veterinary practice can do. Almost any practice in western Europe or North America has the capacity to carry out advanced surgery, radiography, electro-cardiography and other refined veterinary procedures.

Round-the-clock service

Veterinarians in the UK must be on the Royal College of Veterinary Surgeons' Register. They are required by law to provide a service around the clock, every single day of the year. If there are several vets working together in a practice, they will take turns to be on call so that weekends and nights are covered.

Like doctors, vets need to know the work they have to do early in the working day. If you want an appointment (and more so a house call) contact the practice before 10 a.m. – better still, by 9.30. Cases that suddenly become urgent are another matter.

Veterinarians in the United States have office hours every

Above: *Giving a tablet must be done as quickly as possible.*

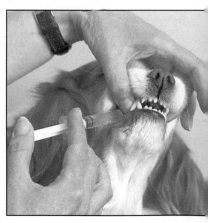

Above: *Liquid medicines can be administered by syringe.*

week day and usually on Saturday. A few may have hours on a limited basis on Sundays. Most require appointments in advance except, of course, in case of emergency. Surgeries for spaying or neutering, teeth cleaning and non-emergency situations often require appointments a week or more in advance.

After hours emergencies may be attended to at Emergency Clinics especially set up for this purpose. Checking with your veterinarian for the clinic nearest

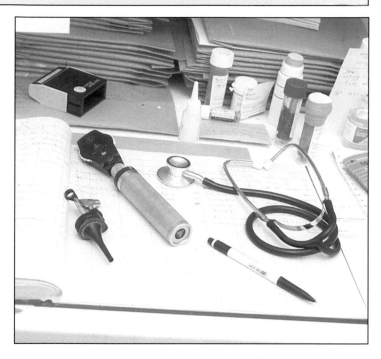

you could save you many anxious moments as well as the life of your pet. Addresses and telephone numbers for these clinics are also listed in the telephone yellow pages.

Most veterinarians in small animal practices no longer make house calls in the United States. A few will, but appointments and agreements must be made well in advance so that no misunderstandings occur. The majority of small animal practitioners feel they are able to give more accurate and complete care at their clinics or hospitals. Again, this is an individual situation between the pet owner and the veterinarians involved.

Types of practice Dogs, even the very largest of them, come under the heading of 'small animals'. This distinguishes them from farm stock and although there are quite a few practices that will attend any domestic animal, most are predominantly either for large or for small ones. (Small animals

Above: *Veterinarians use a wide variety of diagnostic aids.*

are increasingly coming to be known as 'companion animals'.)

Changing your vet If you are not happy with a practice you may change to another, but if you have an animal currently under treatment you must inform the vet of the change: besides being a courtesy, it saves a lot of unnecessary work. The same applies to second opinions. Ask for one with the full knowledge of your vet, and you will prevent a whole range of complications. If a case is proving slow to resolve, you may wish to ask to have it referred to a specialist. Do so by all means, but do not go direct – the specialist cannot act without hearing first from your vet.

Insurance and financial help
Adequate pet insurance has been available in Europe for several years and it makes sense to use it. It does not normally cover

Above: *A routine veterinary check of a puppy begins.*

vaccination or neutering, but most other fees can be included in the policy.

Once your dog is insured, if an accident occurs you can get the best attention without the worry of having to find a lot of money quickly at a time which is already stressful for all the family. There is the additional benefit of being covered for liability in case of any damage your dog may cause to third parties.

In the United States, this kind of health and accident insurance is a very recent innovation and has not been particularly well received in companion animal care circles. There are few American companies in any case who offer this kind of cover, and those that do, tend to limit coverage to accidents resulting in death and/or theft, rather than illness. Professional handlers of show dogs and owners of valuable show and breeding stock may carry such policies. Inquiries to insurance companies, local breed clubs, The American Kennel Club, as well as veterinarians in your area should lead you to this information.

Owners who can give clear proof of financial hardship may, in many countries, seek help from animal welfare societies. If there is clearly going to be a problem with payment, it should be discussed with the charity and with the vet at an early stage.

In the United States, however, it is very rare for welfare agencies to give this kind of aid. Usually it is up to the veterinarian concerned to sort out the problem of payment. Delayed payments or payments on accounts may be made, but this is done on an individual basis. The animal welfare agencies may be able to tell the pet owner which veterinarians they feel would be willing to work with a person unable to afford the necessary care.

Most veterinarians will give an estimate of the likely costs for any case, but it can only be an estimate and not a fixed quotation, unless a special arrangement is made at the outset.

Helping at the examination This normally takes place at the clinic of the local practice, or alternatively it may be in a veterinary hospital. You are usually expected to give some help in lifting the dog and, if necessary, restraining it. On the one hand you are the person most likely to be able to reassure and comfort the animal, and on the other it is your responsibility to warn the veterinary staff if the dog is at all likely to be dangerous.

The veterinarian will normally want to look at many aspects of the dog (whatever it is there for), and most of this will take place without the dog realizing it is under scrutiny.

There is only one other main requirement of you: accurate and concise answers to the veterinarian's questions, plus of course careful attention to the advice he will give.

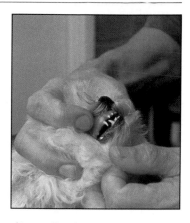

Above: *Teeth and gums are checked as part of the examination procedure.*

Above: *Both ears are very carefully examined by the vet using an auriscope.*

Right: *An ophthalmoscope is used to examine all the parts of the puppy's eyes.*

OLD AGE AND THE END OF LIFE

This book has gone into some detail about the main stages of a dog's life. This has covered puppyhood and growing up, as well as fitting into the family as an adult. However, once a dog has passed into its eighth or ninth year (a year or two earlier for the larger breeds) it can be considered to be ageing.

It is very important, as it is for ourselves, to look upon the final phase of life positively – that is, to make the most of the time there is left. It is pointless to write off what can be very rewarding years of life.

The objective of every owner should be to help in every possible way to keep the dog healthy and happy in its maturity. Much can be done to ease the 'winding down' process and the local veterinarian has a key role to play in keeping the dog as well as possible during this time.

The time will eventually come when such efforts are not effective enough and the dog has to be spared the unpleasant effects of terminal illness. The difficulties of making such decisions have to be faced, but it is possible to make that process easeful and humane.

What is happening to the dog
Ageing is not a specific condition, so each dog will be different. Much will depend on the relative efficiency of each vital system in the body. For example, if the heart and circulation are among the first to be unable to cope, then a different set of clinical signs will be apparent than if it is (say) the nervous sytem. The first has a much better chance of being alleviated with appropriate treatment than the second.

Most older dogs are noticeably less active as the years pass. Their will to do things will wane, and their ability to move about can also soon become restricted. Much can be done to improve mobility by treating arthritis and muscular and other pains. With reduced activity, the actual energy needs of the body are lessened. That is, the dog will need fewer calories.

Food and the ageing dog
Unfortunately, many dogs retain

Below: *Much can be done to ease a dog's declining years.*

the same appetite and so consume more calories than they are using. Because of this, owners have to be watchful for an accumulation of body fat (obesity) which can soon start to have an effect on the dog's life span.

On the other hand some individuals may show a reduced appetite. This may be due to a decrease in the senses, so that the dog can no longer appreciate the sight and smell of food as well as before. Rather stronger smelling foods may be needed to provoke the dog's senses.

Other dogs may actually need more food because their ability to digest and absorb the food they do eat is lessened as they get older.

Dogs frequently require attention to their teeth and gums as deposits accumulate on the teeth and gums soon become inflamed. As this in itself can prevent a dog from eating properly, it is most important for the dog to have continuous dental care. The vet can help, by inspecting, cleaning and polishing the dog's teeth, to keep it able to eat properly every day.

Another effect of ageing on dogs is that the gut may become less motile and so slow down the passage of food. Constipation results, which can make life difficult for the older dog. The transit of food through the gut can be speeded up where necessary by careful use of bulking agents such as bran, as well as lubricants like medicinal liquid paraffin.

Proprietary human laxatives must not be used and advice from the local veterinary practice should always be taken when dogs are constipated.

Veterinary surveillance
It is clear from this that professional advice is needed for almost all aged dogs. This should extend beyond the regular annual check-ups. A veterinarian can assess the dog's health much better if he or she has been the usual attendant on that dog.

The assessment of actual state of health of each organ and each body system is much more effective if it is done on a continuous basis, so that the current state can be compared with function in previous years. This way a veterinarian can determine which body system needs attention and whether more food or less is required.

It may be necessary to return to feeding highly concentrated diets such as a canned puppy food, and to feed many small meals frequently, to allow the dog's digestion to cope. On the other hand when the kidneys begin to fail, it may be necessary to restrict the amount of protein in the diet.

From this it will be clear that the owner cannot know without professional advice whether to feed more or less protein, or whatever other measures are required. As harm can be done by taking the wrong path it is most important to keep an aged dog under veterinary surveillance even when it is otherwise reasonably healthy.

Above: *Many older dogs feel a lot better after attention to their teeth and gums.*

Incontinence

Inability to control the passing of urine and faeces is a common complication of old age. It is always worth investigating, for when it is due to an infection or inflammation of the bladder or gut it is often possible to give effective treatment.

Where there is functional deterioration of the nerve supply or other irreversible change, then it may well be an indication to bring the dog's life to an end.

Bedsores

A dog that is unable to move around freely tends to sink down to rest without much care, and so is liable to wear the skin down where the bones are near the surface. So-called 'bed' or pressure sores are commonly seen on the limbs of older dogs, especially the heavier varieties.

These can be treated with soothing ointments, but it is better to try to avoid them by providing as comfortable a bed as possible, with plenty of cushions and blankets. Such bedding has to be changed and washed frequently, but it is worth making the last years of a dog's life as comfortable as possible.

Above: *A puppy can bring a new lease of life to an old dog.*

Getting another puppy

There is much to be said for getting another puppy as the senior member of the dog household begins to age. This not only helps to make parting a little easier but it can even rejuvenate a dog that is getting a little tired of life but is otherwise healthy.

Managing euthanasia

It is extremely important for owners to take a positive attitude to parting with the pet animal. Veterinarians are privileged to be

---

TABLE 6: QUESTIONS THE VETERINARIAN WILL NEED TO CONSIDER, TO ASSESS THE NEED FOR EUTHANASIA

1) Is the dog free from pain, distress or serious discomfort which cannot be controlled?
2) Is it able to walk freely and balance reasonably well?
3) Is it able to eat and drink enough to maintain its bodyweight without difficulty and without vomiting?
4) Is it free from tumours which cause pain or serious discomfort and are not treatable?
5) Is it able to breathe freely?
6) Is it able to pass urine and faeces without difficulty or incontinence?
7) Is the owner able to cope both physically and emotionally with any nursing likely to be required?

If the answer to any of these questions is 'no' and treatment is not promising, it is likely that the dog is not leading a happy life and there are probably good grounds for euthanasia.

allowed to spare a dog from the unpleasantness of terminal illness. It is easy to deny the need to end a dog's life when the bond of friendship has been so strong, but it is selfish if continuation will bring more suffering for the animal itself.

Regrettably, dogs' lives are short compared with our own, so the pet owner may have to face parting several times in his or her own life, even when the animals live out their usual span. On the other hand dogs should not be disposed of simply because they look a little ancient. What matters is whether they can lead reasonably normal lives and, if they are not doing so, whether anything can be done about it.

Judging these points is far from easy, but it is something veterinarians do practically every day of their lives. They have to ask themselves a number of questions about the case to help them make up their minds. The questions may be quite obvious, but the answers are less so. Table 6 lists some of these questions.

An important point to remember is that the veterinarian is there to advise and cannot force an owner to take his advice. Owners are often reluctant to seek help for fear of being compelled to part with their animal before time.

Unfortunately, this can delay matters so long that the case may become beyond treatment when it could have been helped a little earlier. So owners should always keep in close touch with their vet.

When euthanasia really is necessary, the matter should be discussed fully so that there is no ambiguity. This is quite difficult, as euphemisms for euthanasia are frequently used. 'Putting to sleep' is one to avoid as it can be ambiguous, and tragedies have occurred in the past for want of understanding. The actual process of euthanasia (the word means a good or gentle death) can be explained by the vet.

The humane method is to inject a concentrated solution, as if an anaesthetic was being given, into a vein. This is made even more tranquil by the use of modern premedicants. The difference is that anaesthesia is deepened to the point of no return and the animal dies peacefully and with some dignity.

Coping afterwards

As people develop very strong attachments to their pet animals (it is the reason we keep them after all) there is bound to be a period of difficulty after parting from them. The veterinary practice staff can also help an owner through this phase, if only by reassuring them that the powerful feelings they experience are quite normal and will ease.

The experience is one of bereavement, just as with any other loss in the family. The phases of denial, anger, depression and resolution are well recognized and a little unobtrusive support is usually helpful.

Carrying on

Owners often feel uneasy about getting another puppy when an old dog has passed on. The thought that 'nothing will ever replace him' is strongly felt. If the new puppy is looked upon as carrying on the tradition or even the line, it can be more positive. The new one is not a replacement, but a continuation of a tradition of pet ownership in the family.

Some thought should be given to the choice of time at which to introduce the youngster, as the stage of 'mourning' may not be right. It is not fair on the puppy to start its new life in an atmosphere of anger or denial, but once depression starts to ease it can be of great benefit to everyone to have the attention directed towards bringing up and looking after the new member of the household.

EMERGENCY CARE

This special section gives advice to owners who are confronted with an emergency, for example, if their dog is suddenly taken ill or hit by a car.

Wherever possible the veterinary practice should deal with all accidents and emergencies, right down to the odd cut or abrasion. In cases of emergency, the person calling the veterinary surgery needs to be able to describe accurately what has happened to the dog. A panic-stricken phone call is not much help to the vet.

Sometimes it is obvious that the dog has to be taken straight to the surgery. In these cases it is still important to alert the veterinary staff beforehand.

ESSENTIALS OF FIRST AID
There are two main objectives when you are giving first aid:

1 To stop the situation from getting worse.
Your first actions should always be to remove the immediate cause of the emergency:

- Clear the dog's throat if its airway is blocked.

- Lift a half-drowned dog from the water.

- Switch off the power if the dog appears to have been electrocuted.

- If the emergency is a road accident, remove the injured dog from the road so that it will not be struck by another vehicle.

2 To make the dog as comfortable as possible.
While professional help is being sought – comfort and reassure the animal:

- If the dog is bleeding badly, make some attempt to control the loss of blood.

- Wrap it in a blanket or whatever material there is to hand. In fact it is wise to keep an old (but clean) blanket handy.

- Note that the blanket should not be used in cases of heat stroke.

- If the dog is fairly small, a carrying basket is useful.

FIRST AID KIT
Owners can improve their chances of success by keeping a modest first aid kit in an accessible place in the house or car. This need not be much more than:

- A good supply of dressings, including plenty of bandages of all sizes, absorbent lint and gauze.

- A simple pair of forceps (tweezers).

- A pair of blunt-ended scissors that are *not* used for anything else.

- Something with which to make an improvised muzzle.

- A styptic pencil.

- A dilute solution of hydrogen peroxide.

- A little mustard powder, for use as an emetic (to induce vomiting).

- A tube of soothing ointment.

- Some adhesive plaster.

Include no human medicines.

A STEP BY STEP GUIDE TO FIRST AID
FOR ACCIDENTS AND EMERGENCIES

MAJOR EMERGENCIES

MINOR EMERGENCIES

PUPPY EMERGENCIES

ROAD ACCIDENTS

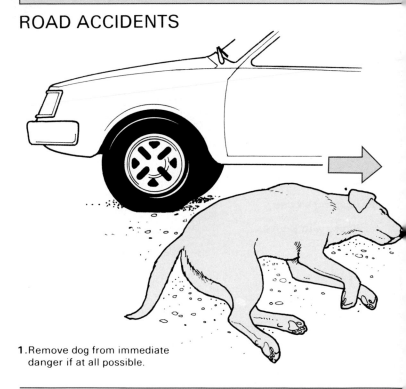

1. Remove dog from immediate
danger if at all possible.

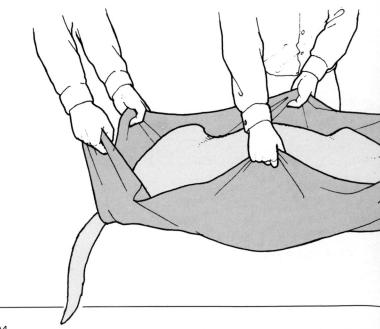

2. Clear airway, maintain breathing, clear all fluids and discharges which may get in the way of breathing.

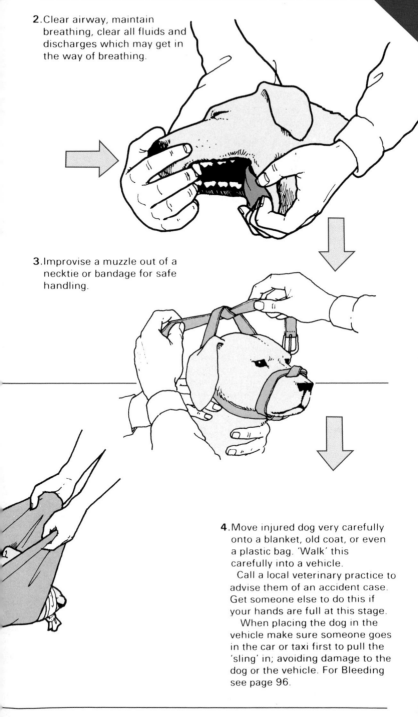

3. Improvise a muzzle out of a necktie or bandage for safe handling.

4. Move injured dog very carefully onto a blanket, old coat, or even a plastic bag. 'Walk' this carefully into a vehicle.

Call a local veterinary practice to advise them of an accident case. Get someone else to do this if your hands are full at this stage.

When placing the dog in the vehicle make sure someone goes in the car or taxi first to pull the 'sling' in; avoiding damage to the dog or the vehicle. For Bleeding see page 96.

MAJOR EMERGENCIES

BLOOD LOSS

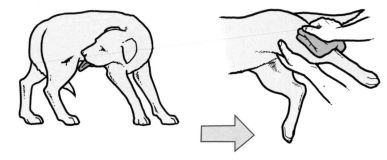

1. Identify main bleeding points. The dog will be licking these.

2. Apply a cold water compress onto the wound first.

BANDAGING A LIMB

1. A clean dressing can be applied on top of a pressure bandage.

2. Care must be taken not to dislodge any blood clots which may form.

3. Apply fresh dressing over the wounded limb with an even distribution.

4. Tie the bandage off, making sure that it does not constrict the limb.

1

COLLAPSE AND SHOCK

1. Keep airway clear. Pull tongue forward and remove any fluid in way of the dog's breathing.

3. Do not allow the dog to lie on one side for more than 10–15 minutes.

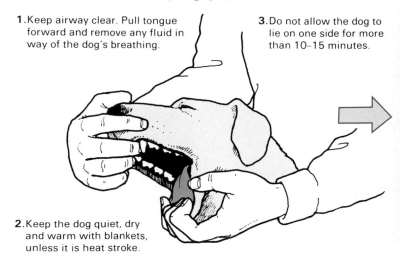

2. Keep the dog quiet, dry and warm with blankets, unless it is heat stroke.

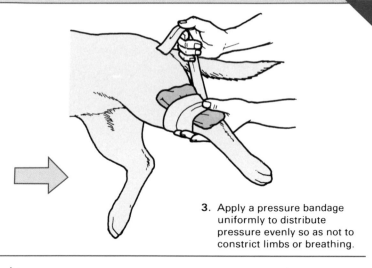

3. Apply a pressure bandage uniformly to distribute pressure evenly so as not to constrict limbs or breathing.

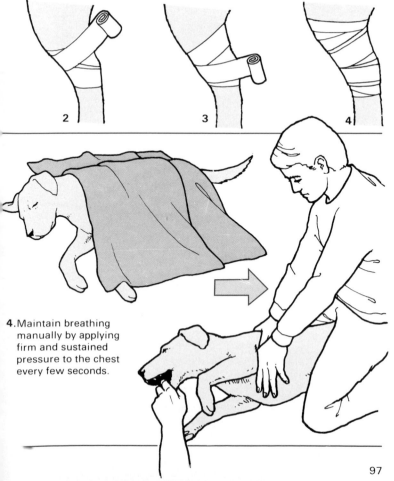

4. Maintain breathing manually by applying firm and sustained pressure to the chest every few seconds.

'BLOAT' (Gastric dilation and torsion)

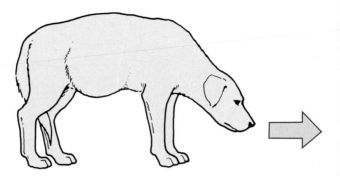

1. 'Bloat' is one of the few really desperate emergencies of dogs. It is caused by a sudden accumulation of gas in the stomach which may cause the stomach to twist.

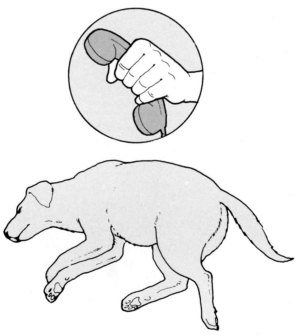

3. Get someone to contact the veterinary surgery while you get the dog to the practice *fast*. Minutes can mean the difference between life and death. With 'bloat' there is very little an owner can do except get the dog to a vet as quickly as possible. The veterinarian will release the gas surgically or by other means. The twisted stomach will be operated on.

2. This twist will trap the gas and the dog will show a sudden severe distension of the abdomen in the flank. It will be in great pain. Collapse follows quickly. If action is not taken immediately the dog will die of heart failure.

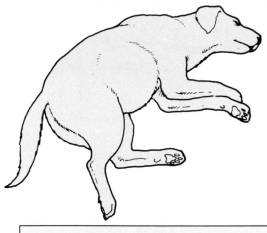

'BLOAT' AFTERCARE

After treatment, try to prevent a possible recurrence of 'bloat' by:

1. Avoiding all excitement at mealtimes.

2. Divide the dog's daily diet into many small meals fed only little and often.

3. Feed with the food bowl in a raised position to reduce the air taken into the stomach. Feed canned foods only.

Keep a constant watch for any signs of recurrence and if so, inform the local veterinary practice immediately whatever time of day it is. For more information see page 76.

MAJOR EMERGENCIES

HEAT STROKE

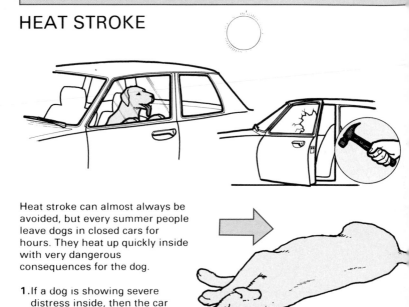

Heat stroke can almost always be avoided, but every summer people leave dogs in closed cars for hours. They heat up quickly inside with very dangerous consequences for the dog.

1. If a dog is showing severe distress inside, then the car may have to be forced open to save the dog's life.

KNOWN POISONING

Poisoning is quite infrequent in dogs. They vomit quite readily which gives them some protection. All the signs of poisoning can be brought about by illnesses which have nothing to do with poisons. Treatment is easier if there are some clues.

1. If the dog is seen to eat something noxious or to swallow human medicines, show the vet what is left.

2. If the dog has not taken anything corrosive then give a solution of salt or soda.

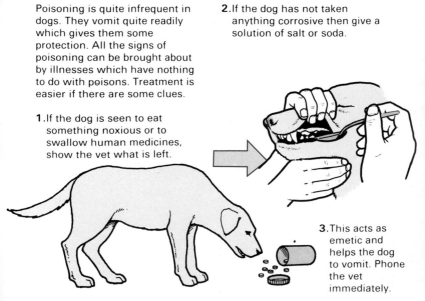

3. This acts as emetic and helps the dog to vomit. Phone the vet immediately.

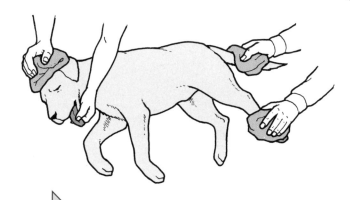

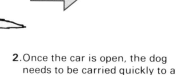

2. Once the car is open, the dog needs to be carried quickly to a cool, shaded, airy place. The dog may be unconscious.

3. Apply cold water compresses to the dog's limbs immediately, or in the case of large dogs, apply cold water direct. A vet should be called while you are doing this. His first action on arrival may be to inject the dog with drugs to reduce the dog's temperature.

FOUR PREVENTABLE POISONING EMERGENCIES

Poison	Present in	Signs of poisoning
Warfarin	Rodent killer, and rodents killed with warfarin	Massive haemhorrages from all openings of the body
Lead	Old, flaky paint	Severe vomiting and diarrhoea
Paraquat	Weed killer	Collapse, great difficulty in breathing
Metaldehyde	Slug pellets, and slugs or snails that have been killed with metaldehyde	Intense overreaction to all stimuli

● **If the dog has been consuming something corrosive, such as acids or solvents, do not induce vomiting. Only the vet can handle this, and it is a serious emergency.**

CHOKING

1. Continuous retching when nothing at all is vomited is a serious sign, especially if the dog is also pawing at its mouth.

ELECTRIC SHOCK

Puppies who are teething occasionally chew through live electric wires. It is always a wise precaution to keep unattended puppies and dogs away from rooms which have live electrical appliances within reach.

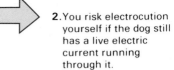

1. If a dog is unconscious and appears to have electrocuted itself, *do not touch the animal* until the current has been switched off from its source and the appliance or wires have been made safe.

2. You risk electrocution yourself if the dog still has a live electric current running through it.

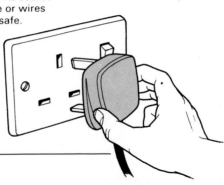

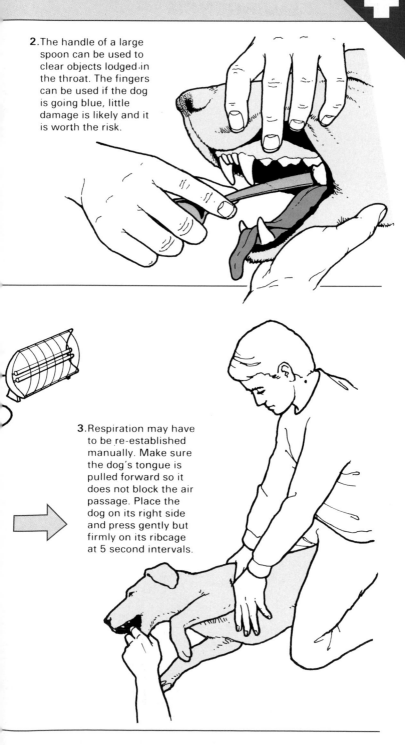

2. The handle of a large spoon can be used to clear objects lodged in the throat. The fingers can be used if the dog is going blue, little damage is likely and it is worth the risk.

3. Respiration may have to be re-established manually. Make sure the dog's tongue is pulled forward so it does not block the air passage. Place the dog on its right side and press gently but firmly on its ribcage at 5 second intervals.

BURNS AND SCALDS

1. Dogs and puppies can easily get scalded or burned from open fires, or pans on stoves.

2. Always put pans away from the edge of the oven and have an efficient guard on fires.

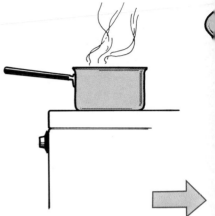

BITES AND STINGS

1. Most bites are from other dogs and always introduce infection. The wound should first be clipped free of hair then bathed with hot water. Look carefully for hidden puncture marks which could later turn to abscesses.

2. Call the veterinarian, as all bitten dogs are usually treated with antibiotic injections. Snake bites are dangerous and are best dealt with by vets.

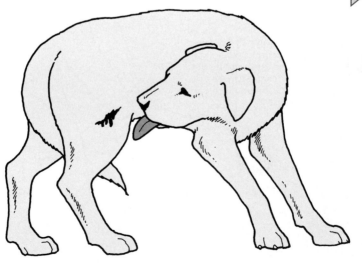

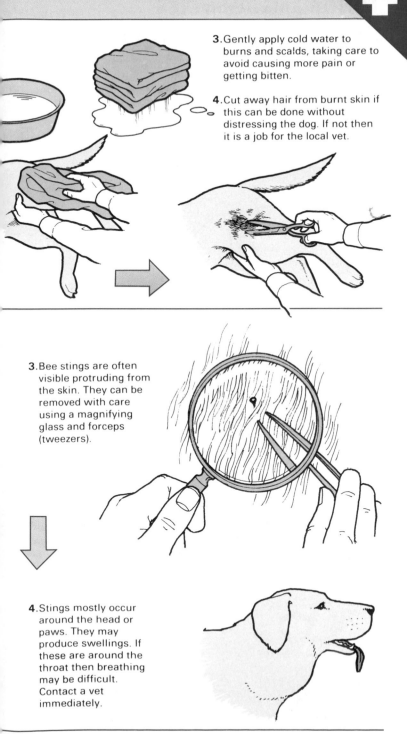

3. Gently apply cold water to burns and scalds, taking care to avoid causing more pain or getting bitten.

4. Cut away hair from burnt skin if this can be done without distressing the dog. If not then it is a job for the local vet.

3. Bee stings are often visible protruding from the skin. They can be removed with care using a magnifying glass and forceps (tweezers).

4. Stings mostly occur around the head or paws. They may produce swellings. If these are around the throat then breathing may be difficult. Contact a vet immediately.

ACUTE VOMITING WITH DIARRHOEA

1. Dogs vomit quite readily and the odd occurrence should not be looked on as dangerous, but if it goes on, it could be serious.

2. Continual vomiting especially with diarrhoea can weaken a dog very quickly and can kill a puppy in a couple of hours.

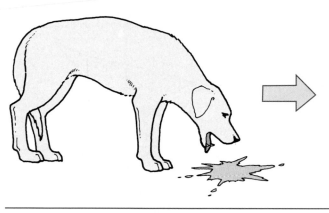

FOREIGN OBJECTS

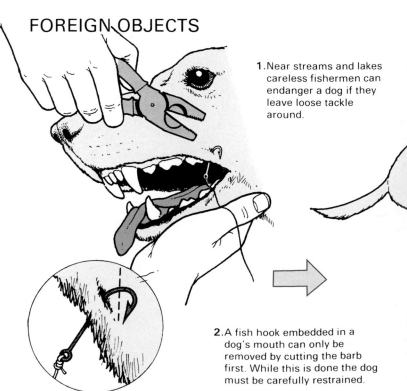

1. Near streams and lakes careless fishermen can endanger a dog if they leave loose tackle around.

2. A fish hook embedded in a dog's mouth can only be removed by cutting the barb first. While this is done the dog must be carefully restrained.

3. In these cases, *never* use human medicines on pet animals. Mechanical mixtures such as kaolin and chalk are acceptable provided they are not vomited back.

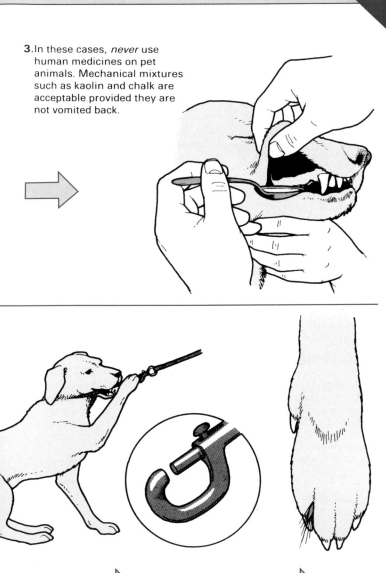

3. Lively, excitable dogs sometimes get the web of their paw caught in the clip of their lead. They are best cut free by a veterinarian.

4. Grass awns can get into feet, ears and eyes. They may cause the dog distress and can lead to abscesses. If embedded deeply removal is best left to a vet.

FOULED COAT

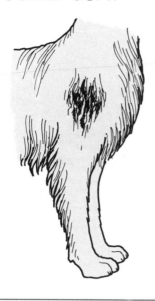

1. Dogs who lead active lives, or those which are simply clumsy, sometimes get their coats fouled with such substances as tar, paint, mud or manure.

2. If the coat cannot be washed with water, then apply butter or lard to soften.

HYPOTHERMIA

1. A dog left outside for a long period in very cold temperatures without shelter may develop hypothermia, which will cause its body temperature to fall to a dangerously low level.

2. Take the dog out of the cold environment immediately, but do not make it very hot very quickly. Insulate the animal with blankets to let its own bodyheat build up. *Do not give any alcohol!*

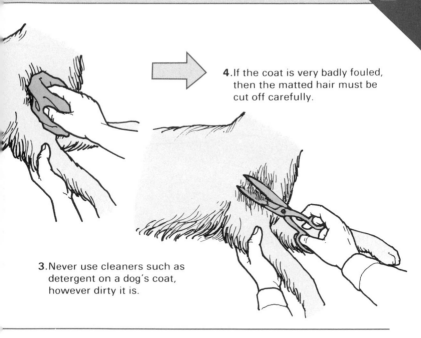

4. If the coat is very badly fouled, then the matted hair must be cut off carefully.

3. Never use cleaners such as detergent on a dog's coat, however dirty it is.

FITS AND SEIZURES

1. Fits often look worse than they actually are. The dog twitches and may froth at the mouth but is not usually conscious.

2. Stop the dog from injuring itself, and don't excite it.

3. Keep the dog in a darkened quiet room until the seizure has passed, then call the vet. Do not expect an immediate visit as fits do not last very long.

DELAY AT BIRTH

1. Do not fuss over a bitch as she goes into whelp, but also do not neglect her. Whelping may go on for 24 hours or even longer.

2. She should not be in unproductive labour for more than an hour, however. If she is, then call for advice.

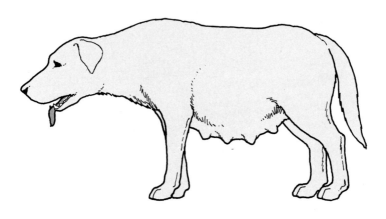

NEARLY BORN PUPPY

1. If a puppy is nearly born, then some careful traction by hand is permissible in the circumstances to invigorate it.

2. With a clean towel apply a firm pull but *no force* to the puppy, downwards and backwards.

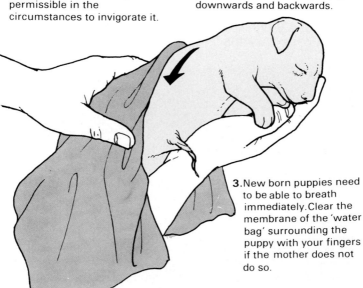

3. New born puppies need to be able to breath immediately. Clear the membrane of the 'water bag' surrounding the puppy with your fingers if the mother does not do so.

3. Help can be given over the phone, but a vet is needed if the puppies do not appear. Alert the practice if it is the first whelp.

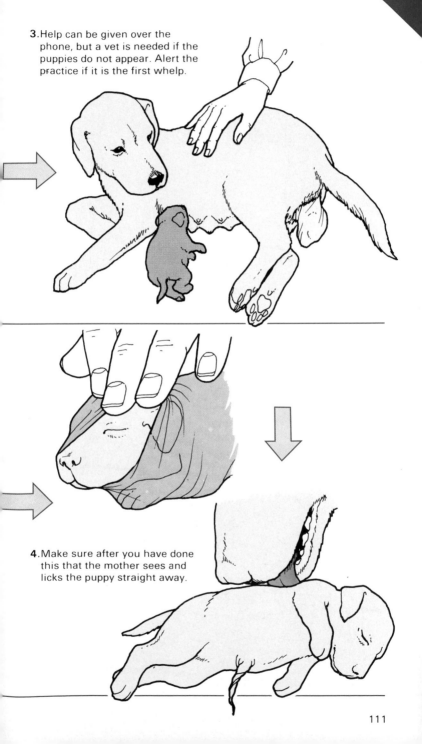

4. Make sure after you have done this that the mother sees and licks the puppy straight away.

PUPPY EMERGENCIES

STILL BORN PUPPY

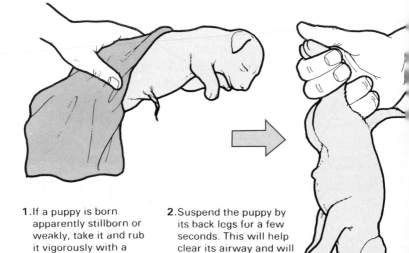

1. If a puppy is born apparently stillborn or weakly, take it and rub it vigorously with a warm dry bath towel. Do not give up.

2. Suspend the puppy by its back legs for a few seconds. This will help clear its airway and will stimulate it to begin breathing

REARING ORPHANED PUPPIES

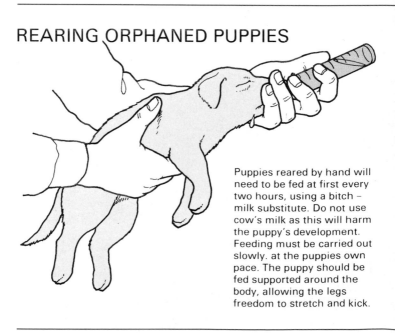

Puppies reared by hand will need to be fed at first every two hours, using a bitch – milk substitute. Do not use cow's milk as this will harm the puppy's development. Feeding must be carried out slowly. at the puppies own pace. The puppy should be fed supported around the body, allowing the legs freedom to stretch and kick.

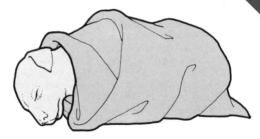

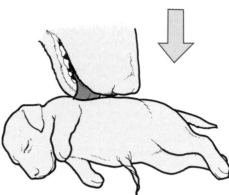

3. Puppies chill easily, so
wrap the puppy in a
blanket or towel and
keep it warm at about
30°C (85°F).

4. After the puppy has
revived a little,
encourage the mother
to lick the puppy
vigorously. This will
stimulate the puppy
and help the two bond.

PUPPY CHECK LIST

3-4 Weeks	Begin supplementing bitch's milk with canned puppy food and milk. Feed to appetite every 3-4 hours during daytime.
5-8 Weeks	Introduce biscuit softened with milk or water to the diet. Feed 3 parts puppy food to 1 part biscuit and milk, every four hours during daytime. Puppies should be fully weaned by 6-7 weeks.
2-4 Months	Divide daily allowance of puppy food/mixer into 4 meals. A vet should be consulted about vaccinations and worming.
4-6 Months	Divide the puppy's food into 3 meals daily.
6-9 Months	Divide the puppy's food into 2 meals daily.

For more information see page 30.

FINDING OUT MORE

Throughout this book there has been a strong emphasis on the need for pet owners to make the best use of their local veterinary practice. The days of veterinary surgeons being consulted only for the odd emergency and for initial vaccinations are past, or at least changes are being made.

The modern veterinarian offers a complete service through his or her practice and its staff. They should all be very approachable for genuine enquiries. It makes good sense to establish a working relationship with a local practice at an early stage, even before the purchase of a dog.

The yellow pages of the telephone directory can be useful to help start your search for a vet; but word of mouth recommendation from experienced pet owners is often a useful guide to the type of practice that is likely to suit a particular owner.

With present-day pet insurance schemes, the cost of veterinary services can be kept under control. There is little excuse for not providing for dogs by pet insurance, and none at all for not protecting a dog by vaccination. At vaccination time there should be every opportunity to discuss feeding, housing, neutering and worming with the attendant veterinarian.

Magazines
There are many magazines and weekly papers, of which *Dog World*, *Our Dogs* and *Dogs' Monthly* are well known in the United Kingdom. The American Kennel Club has an excellent monthly journal, called *American Kennel Gazette*.

Kennel and Cattery Management caters for those interested in every aspect of animal boarding. Similarly, there is a magazine called *Dog Training Weekly* for the competitive side of obedience work.

The Kennel Club in the United Kingdom has a highly respected monthly called the *Kennel Gazette*, which contains a great deal about all dog show activities.

Books
Every major bookshop and public library has at least one shelf devoted to pet keeping in all forms. There is only space here unfortunately to mention just a few dog titles:

Training Your Dog, (Joan Palmer), Salamander Books, London, 1986.
Pet Care (A.T.B. Edney & I.B. Hughes), Blackwell, Oxford, 1986.
The Doglopaedia (J.M. Evans & K. White), Henston, Guildford, 1985.
Choosing and Bringing Up Your Puppy (Kay White), Paperfront, 1975.
How to Have a Well Mannered Dog (Kay White & Jim Evans), Paperfront, 1981.
Dogs: Breeding and Showing (Catherine Sutton), Batsford, London, 1983.
First Aid for Pets (2nd Edition by B.M. Bush), A & C Black, London, 1984.
The Dog Directory (L. Cartledge), published annually by Ryslip Press.
A Dog of Your Own (Jim Allcock), Sheldon Press for the BVA, 1978.
Understanding Your Dog (P.R. Messent), Macdonald, London, 1980.

Below: *Few manage the level of training of this expert sheepdog.*

The Penguin Book of Dogs (R. Caras & M.A. Finalay), Penguin, London, 1981.
Nursing Small Animals & Birds (2nd Edition, Ed. J. Heath), Baillière Tindall, London, 1978.
Jones' Animal Nursing (4th Edition, Ed. D.R. Lane), Pergamon, Oxford, 1986.
All About Your Dog's Health (G.F. West), Pelham Books, London, 1979.
How to Feed Your Dog (W.T. Turner), Popular Dogs, London, 1980.
Handbook of Dog and Cat Nutrition (A.T.B. Edney), Pergamon, Oxford, 1982.
Fit for a Dog (A.D. Walker), Davis Poynter, London, 1980.
The Right Dog For You (D. Tortora), Simon & Shuster, New York, 1980.
Pets Welcome, Herald Advisory Service, London, 1987.

Useful addresses
Royal College of Veterinary Surgeons, 32 Belgrave Square, London SW1X 8QP.
British Small Animal Veterinary Association, 5 St George's Terrace, Cheltenham, Gloucestershire GL50 3PT.
British Veterinary Association, 7 Mansfield Street, London W1M 0AT.
Kennel Club, 1 Clarges Street, London W1Y 8AB.
American Kennel Club, 51 Madison Avenue, New York, NY 10010, USA.
American Animal Hospital

Above: *But fun at home may be just as rewarding.*

Association, PO Box 15899, Denver, Colorado 80215-0899, USA.
American Veterinary Medical Association, 930 North Meacham Road, Schaumburg, Illinois 60196-1074, USA.
Fédération Cynologique Internationale, c/o Rue Léopold II, 14 B-6530 Thuin, Belgium.
Society for Companion Animal Studies, c/o 23 Glengall Road, London SE15 6NJ.
Delta Society (SCAS equivalent in the USA), Century Building, PO Box 1080, Renton, Washington 98057-1080, USA.
People's Dispensary For Sick Animals (PDSA), c/o PDSA House, South Street, Dorking, Surrey RH4 2LB.
Royal Society for the Prevention of Cruelty to Animals (RSPCA), c/o Head Office, Causeway, Horsham, East Sussex.
Petfoods Education Centre, (includes Selectadog Programme) c/o National Office, Freeby Lane, Waltham-on-the-Wolds, Leicestershire LE14 4RS.

Dog training clubs, canine and breed societies Most breeds of dog have at least one breed society looking after their interests; most towns and cities have at least one canine society and dog training club. The national Kennel Club has their names and addresses.

INDEX

A Finnish Spitz and puppy: Finland's national dog